Word

MADE EASY

A beginner's guide including how-to skills and projects

Ewan Arthur

ARCTURUS

This edition published in 2009 by Arcturus Publishing Limited
26/27 Bickels Yard, 151–153 Bermondsey Street,
London SE1 3HA

D1359833

Microsoft product screen shots reprinted with permission from Microsoft Corporation.

Microsoft, Word, Excel, and Windows Vista are trademarks of the Microsoft group of companies.

Word Made Easy is an independent publication and is not affiliated with, nor has it been authorized, sponsored, or otherwise approved by Microsoft Corporation.

Prepared for Arcturus by Starfish Design Editorial and Project Management Ltd.

ISBN: 978-1-84837-304-4
AD001177EN

Printed in China

Contents

How to use this book

This book will help you learn how to use Microsoft **Word**, probably the most popular word processor in the world.

- It is written for beginners and covers only what you really need.

- There's no jargon, just simple instructions and lots of pictures. You'll start with the basics and soon be able to write letters, design posters and add pictures.

- Every left hand page is called *How to do it* and teaches a new skill. Every right hand page is called *Using it* and has a fun exercise to practise that skill.

HOW TO DO IT

This explains each skill and the steps needed to use the skill. Pictures show you what's on your computer screen.

USING IT

These exercises make up a series of projects. The *Using it* pages also have simple step-by-step stages with pictures.

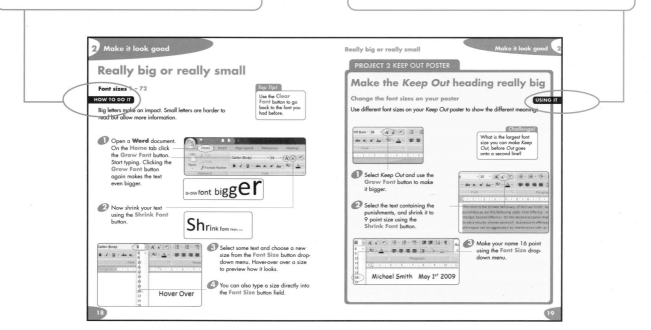

The Microsoft Office **Word** window

What you will see when you open **Word**:

The **Office** button. Click this to do things to the whole document such as save it. You can also customise how **Word** works.

The **Ribbon** – is where most of the options that you will learn about are found.

The **Quick Access Toolbar** – does most of the very common tasks such as Open and Save, but without any options.

The **Close** button. Click to exit **Word**.

The **Horizontal ruler** – shows you the text edges on the document.

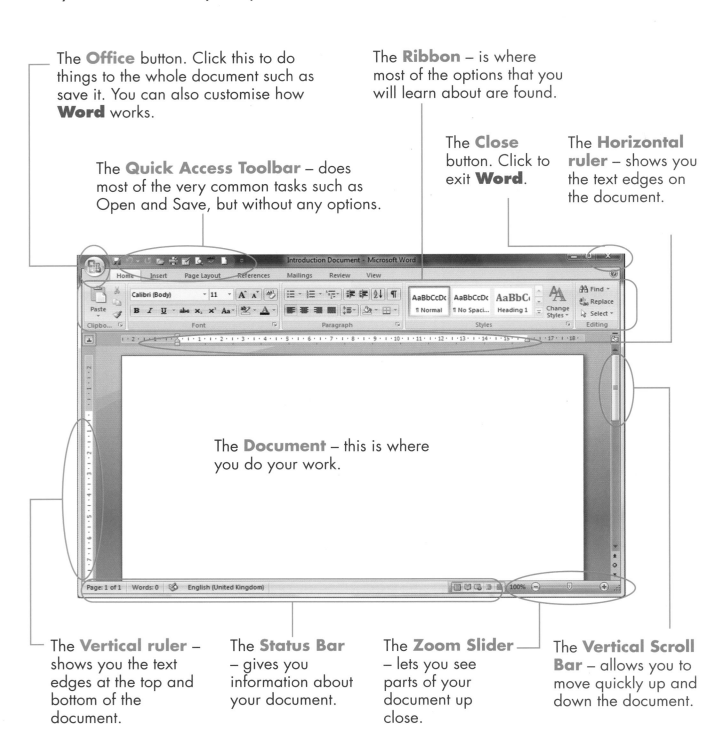

The **Document** – this is where you do your work.

The **Vertical ruler** – shows you the text edges at the top and bottom of the document.

The **Status Bar** – gives you information about your document.

The **Zoom Slider** – lets you see parts of your document up close.

The **Vertical Scroll Bar** – allows you to move quickly up and down the document.

The ribbon

The **ribbon** is where to find most of the tools you use. The ribbon is divided into **tabs**. Each tab is split up into sets of tools. **Word** is clever and depending on what you are doing, puts useful tabs in the ribbon.

A **Button**.

A **Button Drop-down Menu** – shows options related to a button.

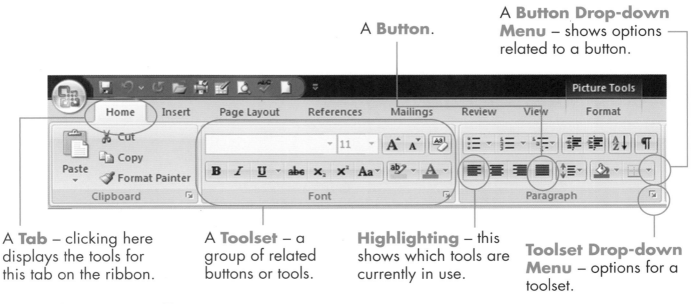

A **Tab** – clicking here displays the tools for this tab on the ribbon.

A **Toolset** – a group of related buttons or tools.

Highlighting – this shows which tools are currently in use.

Toolset Drop-down Menu – options for a toolset.

Starting **Word**

What to do to get **Word** running on your computer.

1 Click the **Start** button.

2 Select **All Programs**.

3 Select **Microsoft Office**. If you can't see this, click-and-drag the scroll bar on the right until you can.

4 Select **Microsoft Office Word**.

Using the mouse

You will use a mouse and keyboard with **Word**. You can often use either to do the same thing. For example, get help by pressing the **F1** function key or clicking on the (?) icon.

Common terms and techniques

Right-click – press and release the <u>right</u> hand button.

Click – press and release the <u>left</u> hand button.

Click-and-drag – press the left mouse button, move (or drag) the cursor, then release it. This either highlights everything covered or moves whatever was selected by the first click.

Mouse pointer – moving the mouse moves the mouse pointer around the screen. It changes depending on what is going on.

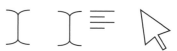

Cursor – The flashing line (cursor) shows where type will appear when entered.

Hover-over – keep the mouse pointer over a button for a few seconds. This will often produce a pop-up message.

Using the keyboard

Common terms and techniques

Esc – closes any pop-up windows you don't want anymore.

Caps Lock – when pressed, everything is typed in capital letters.

Function Keys – can be used as shortcuts for tools and options. The **F7** key starts the spelling checker.

Backspace – deletes text to the <u>left</u> of the cursor.

Delete – deletes text to the <u>right</u> of the cursor.

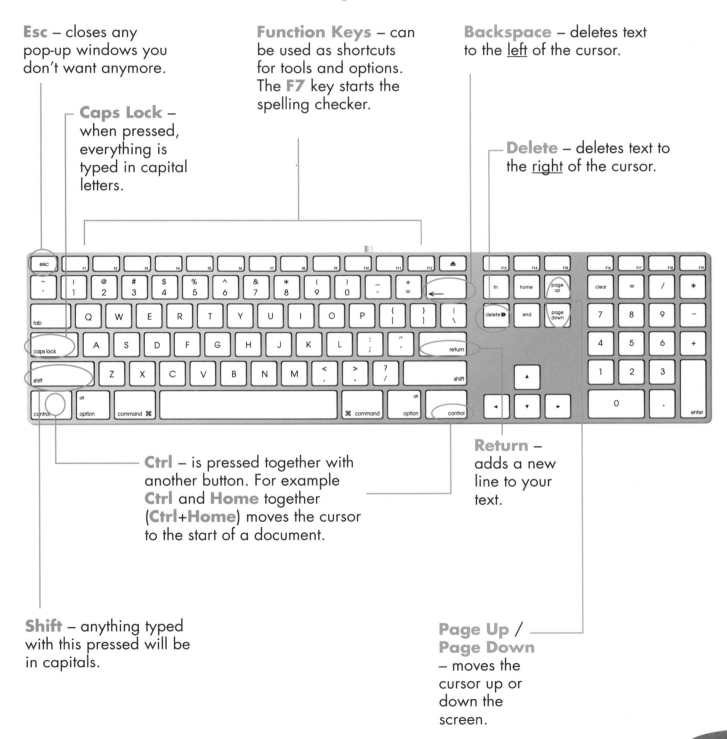

Ctrl – is pressed together with another button. For example **Ctrl** and **Home** together (**Ctrl+Home**) moves the cursor to the start of a document.

Return – adds a new line to your text.

Shift – anything typed with this pressed will be in capitals.

Page Up / Page Down – moves the cursor up or down the screen.

Starting **Word**

The **Office** button, **New** and **Save**

HOW TO DO IT

Using **Word**, you will need to make and save new documents.

1 Click the **Office** button at the top left of your screen.

2 Select **New**. The 'New Document' dialog box appears. Double-click **Blank Document** for a new document.

3 Type your address.

4 To save the document, click the **Office** button.

5 Select **Save**.

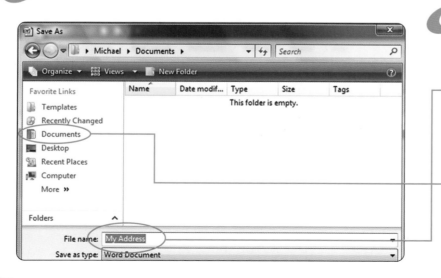

6 The 'Save As' dialog box pops up. Give your document the file name *My Address*. Put it into a folder to organise your documents. The default folder is *Documents*.

PROJECT 1 FIRST STEPS

Start your first **Word** document

Open a new document, type your name and address and save it

USING IT

An easy first step.

1 Open a new document.

2 Type your name.

3 Press the **Enter** key.

4 Type your address. Press the **Enter** key after each line. Add your country.

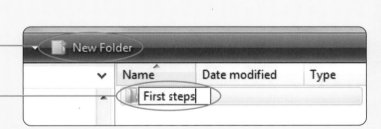

5 Save your work. Click the **New Folder** button and name it *First steps*. Then save your document as *First steps 1*.

6 Close **Word** by clicking the **Close** button in the top right corner of the screen.

Opening and closing existing documents

The **Office** button, **Open** and **Save As**

HOW TO DO IT

You have created your first **Word** document. You may want to copy it with a different name so the original is still available.

1 Click the **Office** button and select **Open**.

2 You will see the 'Open' dialog box. This opens in the *Documents* folder unless you have already opened another folder.

3 Find the file you want.

4 Click the **Office** button.

5 Select **Save As**.

6 Save the document with a new name.

PROJECT 1 FIRST STEPS

Open your saved document

Open *First steps 1* and save it as *First steps 2*

USING IT

Create two versions of *First steps* so you don't lose the original.

1 Click the **Office** button then select **Open** to find *First steps 1*. Open it.

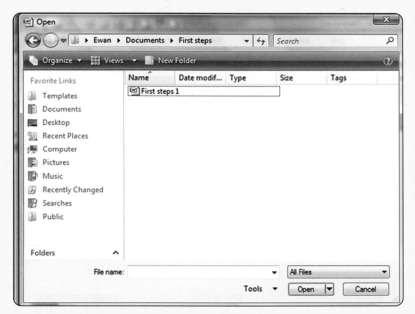

2 Click the **Office** button, select **Save As** and rename it *First Steps 2*.

3 Type the date into *First Steps 2* and save it.

4 Close **Word** by clicking the **Close** button.

Moving around a **Word** document

The **Mouse**, the **Keyboard** and your **Document**

HOW TO DO IT

You will need to move around your document to change things or correct mistakes.

> This is where the cursor is | but it should be flashing.

1 To add text to a different part of the document, move the mouse pointer and click or use the **Arrow** keys.

> This is the mouse pointer when it is over ⌶ text.

2 If you can't see the part where you want to type, click-and-drag the 'Scroll Bar' or use the **Page Up** and **Page Down** keys.

3 Use the **Backspace** key to delete text to the <u>left</u> of the cursor, or the **Delete** key to delete text to the <u>right</u>.

> This is a block of text that has been selected using click-and-drag

4 To delete a lot of text, click-and-drag the mouse pointer across the text, then press the **Delete** key.

Top Tip!

Ctrl + Home moves the cursor to the top of the document; **Ctrl + End** to the end. **Ctrl + A** selects everything.

PROJECT 1 FIRST STEPS

Add your birth date after your name and delete your country

USING IT

Change *First steps 2*

Now that we have two versions of *First steps*, we can play with one and keep the original.

> **Top Tip!**
>
> You can use the **Start** button and select **Recent Items** to open your document without starting **Word** first.

1 Open *First steps 2*.

> Michael M. Ouse
>
> 10210 Princess Parkway

2 Move the mouse pointer to the end of your name and click.

3 Type your date of birth and press the **Return** key.

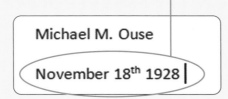

> Michael M. Ouse
>
> November 18th 1928 |

4 Move the mouse pointer to the start of your country.

5 Click-and-drag over the words to select them.

> United States of Disney

6 Delete this selection by pressing the **Delete** key.

Zooming in and out

Setting Zoom on the page so you can read your work

HOW TO DO IT

You may want your work to appear bigger or smaller on the screen without changing its size on the printed page.

1 Click the **View** tab.

2 Click the **Zoom** button. The 'Zoom' dialog box appears.

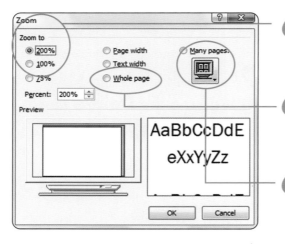

3 To make the document really big, select '200%' then click **OK**.

4 To fit the whole page onto your screen, select 'Whole page'.

5 To see several pages at once, select the 'Many pages' option.

6 To make the document fit the screen <u>width</u>, click the **View** tab then the **Page Width** button.

PROJECT 1 FIRST STEPS

Find the perfect zoom

Adjust the zoom so you can see as much of your page as possible

USING IT

Even if you only have a small document, it is still good to explore the different **View** options.

1 In *First steps 1*, set the page to full page width.

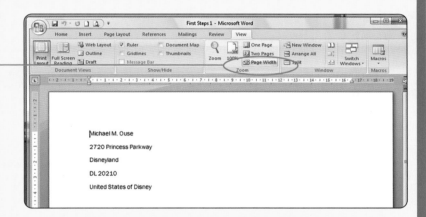

2 Note the size on the status bar.

3 Use the **Zoom** button to show 'Whole page' and note the new size on the status bar.

4 Use the **Zoom** button to change the view size percentage. Try *72%*.

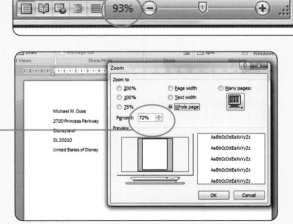

Different styles of text

Fonts from *Arial* to *Wingding3*

One way to change your document look is to change the <u>font</u>. This is the letter style of text. Each font has a name, e.g. *Times New Roman*.

1 Open a new **Word** document.

2 Click the **Font** drop-down menu. A list of fonts appears.

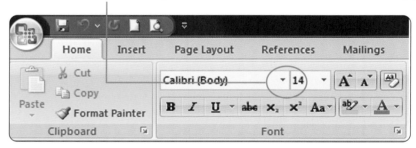

This line of text is in Times New Roman

This line of text is in Elephant

This line of text is in Bradley Hand ITC

3 Type and select some new text. Select a new font. Try *Elephant*.

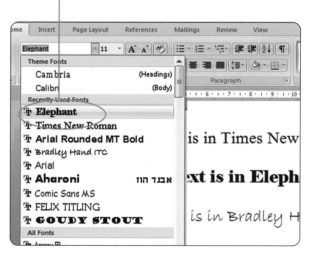

4 Type more text. Select it.

5 Click the **Font** drop-down menu and try *Bradley Hand ITC*.

Top Tip!

Select some text in a document, click the **Font** selector and hover-over a font name to see what your text will look like.

PROJECT 2 KEEP OUT POSTER

Use different fonts in your poster

Explore different fonts to help your poster stand out

Different fonts can be used for different purposes. Fonts can look serious, business-like, old-fashioned or fun.

1 Create a document called *Keep Out Poster*.

2 Type the heading *Keep Out*.

3 Add two blank lines then type some text about the punishments for not keeping out of your room.

Keep Out

This room is the private sanctuary of Michae
offence punishable as per the following scale
time will be given a Wedgie. Second Offence
trespassing, the offender will be made to eat
punishable by six weeks washing up dishes a
or removal of the goods and chattels contain

Michael Smith   May 1st 2009

4 Press the **Enter** key twice, change the font to *Comic Sans MS* then type your name and the date.

5 Now change the font for *Keep Out* to **Arial Rounded MT Bold.**

Really big or really small

Font sizes 1 – 72

HOW TO DO IT

Big letters make an impact. Small letters are harder to
read but allow more information.

1 Open a **Word** document. On the **Home** tab click the **Grow Font** button. Start typing. Clicking the **Grow Font** button again makes the text even bigger.

2 Now shrink your text using the **Shrink Font** button.

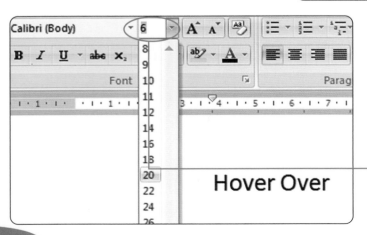

3 Select some text and choose a new size from the **Font Size** button drop-down menu. Hover-over over a size to preview how it looks.

4 You can also type a size directly into the **Font Size** button field.

PROJECT 2 KEEP OUT POSTER

Make the *Keep Out* heading really big

Change the font sizes on your poster

USING IT

Use different font sizes on your *Keep Out* poster to show the different meanings.

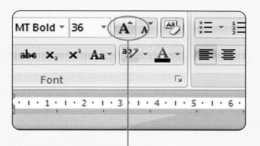

Challenge!

What is the largest font size you can make *Keep Out*, before *Out* goes onto a second line?

1 Select *Keep Out* and use the **Grow Font** button to make it bigger.

2 Select the text containing the punishments, and shrink it to 9 point size using the **Shrink Font** button.

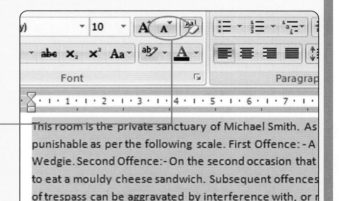

This room is the private sanctuary of Michael Smith. As punishable as per the following scale. First Offence: - A Wedgie. Second Offence: - On the second occasion that to eat a mouldy cheese sandwich. Subsequent offences of trespass can be aggravated by interference with, or r

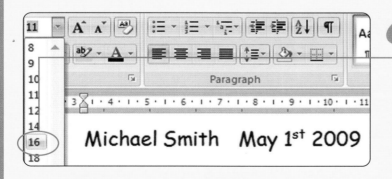

Michael Smith   May 1st 2009

3 Make your name 16 point using the **Font Size** drop-down menu.

Where does the text go?

Aligning lines of text

HOW TO DO IT

Word automatically aligns lines of text to the <u>left</u>, but you may want the text to appear on the right or in the middle of the page.

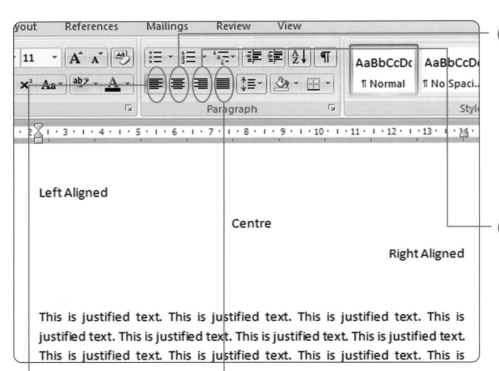

1 Select some text. On the **Home** tab in the 'Paragraph' toolset, click the **Center** button. The line moves to the centre of the page.

2 Click the **Align Text Right** button. The line moves to the right edge.

3 Click the **Justify** button. Text spreads to touch both edges of the page.

4 Click the **Align Text Left** button. The line shifts back to touch the left edge.

PROJECT 2 KEEP OUT POSTER

Centre your heading on page

Align the different parts of your poster in different ways

Your poster is currently aligned to the left. Align the text in different ways to make it look better.

1 Select the *Keep Out* heading and make it centre aligned.

Keep Out

This room is the private sanctuary of Michael Smith. As such, entry without prior permission is an offence punishable as per the following scale. First Offence: - A person caught trespassing for the first time will be given a Wedgie. Second Offence:- On the second occasion that a person is caught trespassing, the offender will be made to eat a mouldy cheese sandwich. Subsequent offences shall be punishable by six weeks cleaning dishes. The offence of trespass can be aggravated by interference with, or removal of the goods and chattels contained herein.

Michael Smith May 1st 2009

2 Select the next block of text and justify the text.

3 Select your name and right align it.

Space out your text

Use **Line Spacing** and **Indents**

Remember!
Settings from the
'Paragraph' toolset apply to
the <u>whole</u> paragraph.

HOW TO DO IT

You can change your document look by increasing space between lines of text or
changing where text starts on a line.

1 From the 'Paragraph' toolset of the
Home tab, click the **Line Spacing**
button drop-down menu.

2 Select **1.5**. The space between lines of
text becomes one-and-a-half times as big.

3 Select **2.0**. The space between lines is
now <u>double</u> normal size.

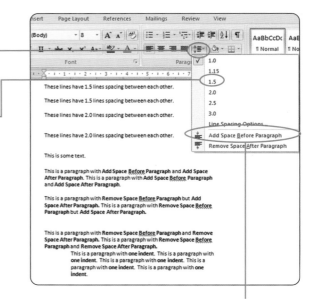

4 Select **Add Space Before
Paragraph**.

5 The default setting is a space
after paragraphs. Select
**Remove Space After
Paragraph** to remove it.

Top Tip!
Click the
'Paragraph' toolset
drop-down menu to
explore more
options.

6 Click the **Increase Indent**
button to start the paragraph
further into the page.

PROJECT 2 KEEP OUT POSTER

Space out the poster punishments text

Adding space between the lines of your text will make it easier to read

USING IT

Your *Keep Out* poster needs to be really clear.

1 Select a block of text and give it a line spacing of *1.5*.

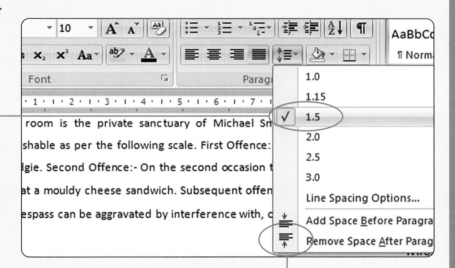

This room is the private sanctuary of Michael Sm
punishable as per the following scale. First Offence:
Wedgie. Second Offence:- On the second occasion tl
to eat a mouldy cheese sandwich. Subsequent offenc
of trespass can be aggravated by interference with, o

This is my solemn promise

Michael Smith   May 1st 2009

2 Remove the space after the paragraph. Add a new line to the end of the block of text.

3 Add 3 indents then type *This is my solemn promise*.

Add a splash of colour

Remember!

Typing changes everything from the 'cursor' onwards, or type over any text you have selected.

Change text **colour**

HOW TO DO IT

Word can create really colourful work.

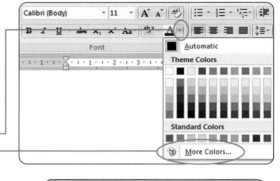

1 Type and select some text in a new document.

2 From the 'Font' toolset of the **Home** tab, click the **Font Color** button drop-down menu.

3 Select a green from the **Standard** tab.

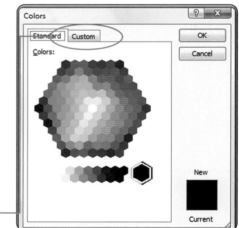

4 Click the **Font Color** button and select **More Colors**. Choose a pink. Click **OK**. The text has changed colour again.

5 Click the **Font Color** button and select **More Colors**. Click the **Custom** tab.

6 Click in the 'Colors' area to choose a colour. Click-and-drag on the 'Brightness Bar' handle to lighten or darken the colour. You can see how your colour changes.

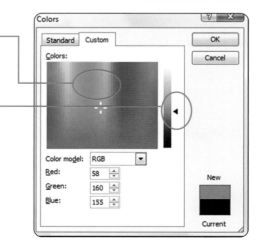

PROJECT 2 KEEP OUT POSTER

Make your text stand out

Make the different parts of your poster different colours

Your *Keep Out* poster needs to be really clear.

Challenge!

Use **Custom Colors** to find your favourite colour and use that.

1 Select *Keep Out* and make it <u>red</u>.

2 Select the main block of text and make it a <u>dark blue</u> from the standard colours.

Keep Out

This room is the private sanctuary of Michael Smith. As such, entry without prior permission is an offence punishable as per the following scale. First Offence: - A person caught trespassing for the first time will be given a Wedgie. Second Offence:- On the second occasion that a person is caught trespassing, the offender will be made to eat a mouldy cheese sandwich. Subsequent offences shall be punishable by six weeks cleaning dishes. The offence of trespass can be aggravated by interference with, or removal of the goods and chattels contained herein.

This is my solemn promise.

Michael Smith May 1st 2009

3 Select one of your punishments and make it bright green in colour.

4 Highlight another punishment and make it the same colour.

5 Select your name and make it a custom colour.

Add some emphasis

Text styles: Bold, Italics, Underline and Strikethrough

HOW TO DO IT

Text styles are another way of making text interesting and emphasising your document.

1 From the 'Font' toolset in the **Home** tab, click the **Bold** button.

2 Use the **Italics** button to italicise text.

3 Click on the **Underline** button to underline text.

4 Click the **Underline** button drop-down menu to see and use other underlines.

5 Using the **Strikethrough** button crosses out your text.

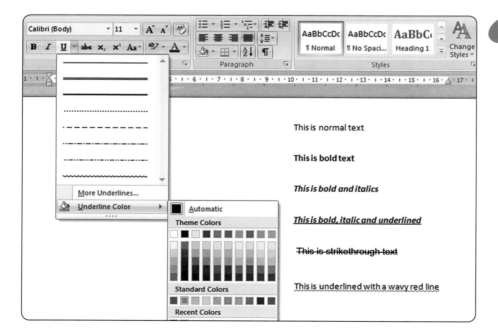

This is normal text

This is bold text

This is bold and italics

This is bold, italic and underlined

This is strikethrough text

This is underlined with a wavy red line

Top Tip!

You can mix all options, e.g. making text bold, italic and underlined.

PROJECT 2 KEEP OUT POSTER

Emphasise your poster's punishments

Let text styles show people you mean business

USING IT

Using text styles will emphasise parts of your poster.

1 Select *Keep Out* and make it bold.

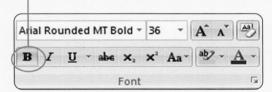

2 Use a wavy underline for your oath. Change the underline colour.

This is my solemn promise.

3 Make all of your punishment text italics.

This room is the private sanctuary of Michael Smith. As such, entry with punishable as per the following scale. First Offence: - A person caught trespas *Wedgie 2 Wedgies.* Second Offence:- On the second occasion that a person is be made to eat a *mouldy cheese sandwich.* Subsequent offences shall be punis offence of trespass can be aggravated by interference with, or removal of the g

4 Strike through a gruesome punishment and add a more gruesome one.

Highlighting text

Use the **Text Highlight Color** button

Remember!

Click-and-drag over text to select it.

HOW TO DO IT

Highlighting attracts the reader's attention to important information.

1 The **Highlighter** button only works on selected text.

2 Click the **Text Highlight Color** button to switch it on.

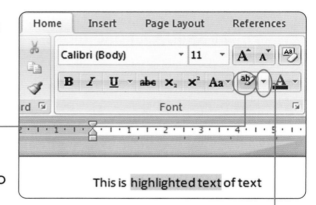

This is highlighted text of text

3 Click-and-drag over the text you want to highlight.

Top Tip!

A dark highlight requires a light font colour.

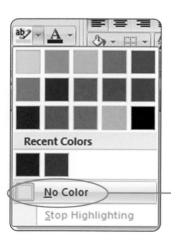

4 Click the **Text Highlight Color** button again to turn the highlighter off, or press the **Escape** key.

5 To use a new colour, click the **Highlighter** button drop-down menu and choose a new colour.

6 To remove highlighting from text, select it and choose **No Color** from the **Highlighter** button drop-down menu.

PROJECT 2 KEEP OUT POSTER

Highlight your poster's oath

Highlighting is another way of emphasising your poster

Your poster is now looking busy. Highlight text to make it stand out from the other colours.

1 Select your oath and highlight it (the colour will be default yellow).

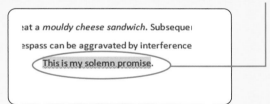

2 Change the highlight colour to dark yellow and highlight your signature line.

3 Change the highlight colour to black and highlight something too gruesome to be read.

4 Change the highlight colour to **No Color** and <u>remove</u> the highlighting from your oath.

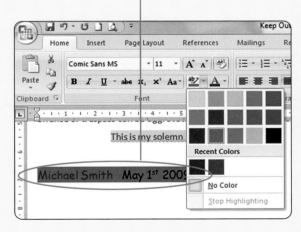

Other emphasis options

Style text using **Borders** and **Shading**

HOW TO DO IT

You can use paragraph shading and borders to colour whole paragraphs in one go.

1 Click into a paragraph on a document.

2 From the **Home** tab 'Paragraph' toolset, click the **Shading** button drop-down menu.

3 Select the colour you want. The background of the whole paragraph changes.

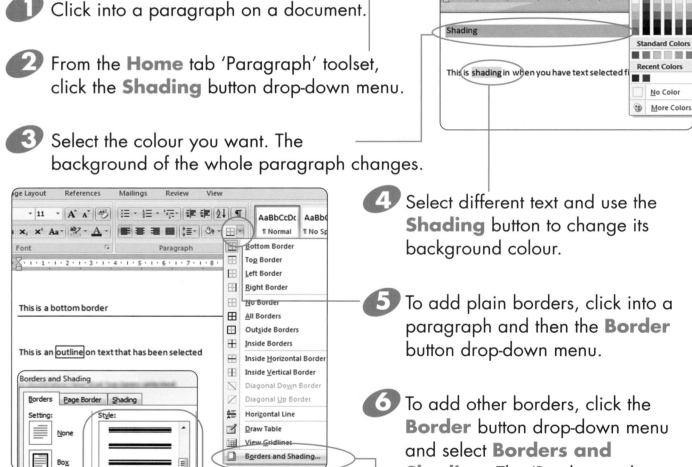

4 Select different text and use the **Shading** button to change its background colour.

5 To add plain borders, click into a paragraph and then the **Border** button drop-down menu.

6 To add other borders, click the **Border** button drop-down menu and select **Borders and Shading**. The 'Borders and Shading' dialog box appears.

7 You can change the style and colour of the border.

PROJECT 2 KEEP OUT POSTER

Put the *Keep Out* heading on a dark background

USING IT

Add borders and shading to your poster

Use borders and shading to divide your poster into different sections.

1 Select your oath and add a bottom border.

2 Select *Keep Out* and apply a background shade.

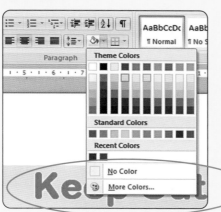

Challenge!

In **Borders and Shading** there are 'Settings' on the left hand side. What do these do?

3 Select some punishments text and bring up the 'Borders and Shading' dialog box.

4 Select a plain border style, grey colour and set the width to 3pt.

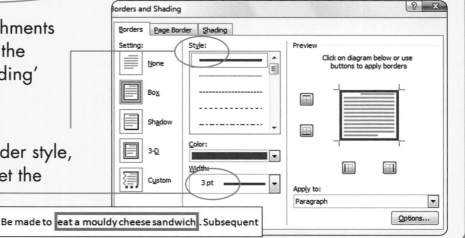

Bust a CAPITAL!

Use the **chAnGE CASE** options

HOW TO DO IT

Word automatically starts a sentence with a capital letter, but there are other possibilities.

1 You can only change the 'Case' of existing text.

2 In the 'Font' toolset on the **Home** tab, click the **Change Case** button drop-down menu.

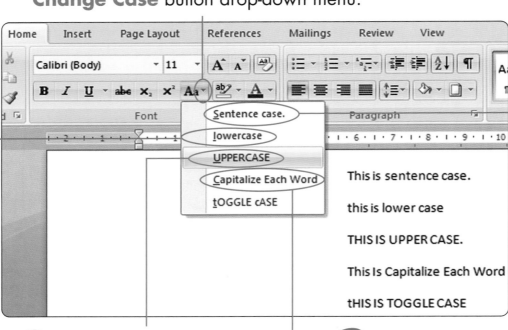

3 Select **UPPERCASE** for all capital letters.

4 For all normal letters, select **lowercase**.

5 To put a capital at the start of each word, use **Capitalise Each Word**.

6 To get capitalisation back to normal, use **Sentence case**.

PROJECT 2 KEEP OUT POSTER

Change the *Keep Out* heading to *KEEP OUT*

USING IT

Using uppercase is like SHOUTING

The **Change Case** button is very useful if you have made a mistake.

1 On your poster document, select *Keep Out* and make it uppercase.

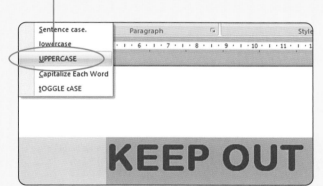

2 Select the first sentence and capitalise each word.

This room is the private sanctuary of Michael Smith.

This Room Is The Private Sanctuary Of Michael Smith.

3 Highlight the main text and make it all sentence case.

4 Make your oath lowercase.

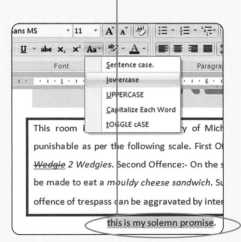

2 Make it look good

The latest styles

Remember!

Hover-over a style to see what it will look like.

Using the **Text Styles** in **Word**

HOW TO DO IT

Styles are pre-set combinations of 'Fonts', 'Font sizes', and 'Colours'. Using styles keeps your **Word** document consistent. If you change the settings for a style, the text in your document changes wherever that style has been used.

1 Select a paragraph.

| AaBbCcDc Emphasis | AaBbCcDc Intense E... | **AaBbCcDc** Strong | AaBbCcDc Quote | *AaBbCcDc* Intense Q... | AABBCCDC Subtle Ref... | AABBCCDC Intense R... | **AABBCCDC** Book Title | Change Styles |

Styles

2 From the **Home** tab, click the 'Book Title' style.

Title Style

Heading 1 Style

This is a block of text with the INTENSE REFERENCE style

3 That style is now applied to the <u>paragraph</u>.

4 Select some text and another style. That style is applied to the <u>text</u>.

Top Tip!

To clear all styling, select **Clear Formatting** from the 'Styles' toolset drop-down menu.

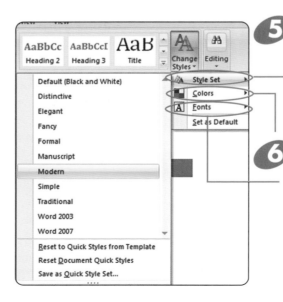

| AaBbCc Heading 2 | AaBbCcI Heading 3 | AaB Title | Change Styles | Editing |

- Default (Black and White)
- Distinctive
- Elegant
- Fancy
- Formal
- Manuscript
- Modern
- Simple
- Traditional
- Word 2003
- Word 2007
- Reset to Quick Styles from Template
- Reset Document Quick Styles
- Save as Quick Style Set...

- Style Set
- Colors
- Fonts
- Set as Default

5 The **Change Styles** button drop-down menu gives you options to change the styling of your <u>whole</u> document.

6 Select **Style Set**, **Colors** or **Font** to alter the 'Styles' in the current 'Set'. All existing styles will change and your document will look totally different.

Apply styles to your poster

Use styles to make your poster look professional

USING IT

Different styles have different names. Explore how they look.

KEEP OUT

This room is the private sanctuary of Michael Smith. punishable as per the following scale. First Offence: - A ~~Wedgie~~ 2 Wedgies. Second Offence:- On the second o will be made to ea a *mouldy cheese sandwich cleaning dishes*. The offence of trespass can be aggr chattels contained herein.

this is my solemn promise.

1. Select *KEEP OUT* and apply the 'Title' paragraph style.

2. Select your oath and apply the 'Strong' paragraph style.

3. Select your punishments and apply the 'Intense Emphasis' paragraph style.

4. Change to the *Formal* document 'Style Set'.

5. Change to the *Verve* document 'Colors' set.

6. Change to the *Trek* document 'Fonts' set.

KEEP OUT

This room is the private sanctuary of Michael Smith. As such, entry punishable as per the following scale. First Offence: - A person caug given a ~~Wedgie~~ 2 **WEDGIES**. Second Offence:- On the second occasi the offender will be made to eat a ***MOULDY CHEESE SANDWICH.*** by ***SIX WEEKS CLEANING DISHES***. The offence of trespass can be aggr of the goods and chattels contained herein.

THIS IS MY SOLEMN PROMISE.

Michael Smith May 1st 2009

Make your own style

Adding a **New Style** to the **Styles** toolset

HOW TO DO IT

The 'Styles' built into **Word** give you a wide range of document looks, but they won't meet all needs.

1 Open a document and select a paragraph of text.

2 Change the 'Font' and 'Paragraph' settings to how you want your new style to look.

> THIS IS MY NEW STYLE
> FELIX TITLING 16PT WITH 3PT BLUE BOTTOM BORDER

3 Click the **Change Styles** button drop-down menu.

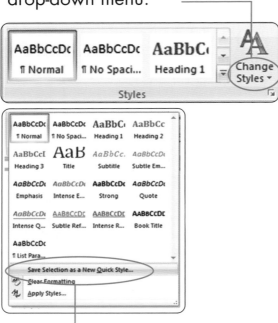

5 Give your new style the name *Green Felix16*. This now appears in the 'Styles' toolset.

4 Select **Save Selection as a New Quick Style**.

PROJECT 2 KEEP OUT POSTER

Add the *KEEP OUT* heading style to your styles toolset

USING IT

Save your *KEEP OUT* heading style

Using Styles has made your poster look very professional, but a little boring.

1 Select the *KEEP OUT* heading text.

2 Double the font size. Change the colour to make it brighter.

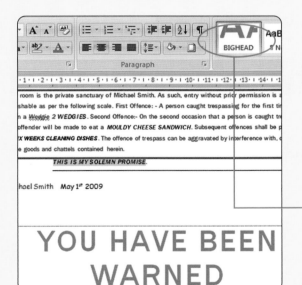

3 Save these settings as a **New Quick Style**.

4 Click on the bottom of your document and type the new line, *YOU HAVE BEEN WARNED*.

5 Apply your new style to this line.

Check before printing

Remember!

Print Preview is also available in the 'Quick Access' toolbar.

Using **Print Preview**

HOW TO DO IT

'Print Preview' is how you check what your document will look like when printed.

1 Click the **Office** button.

2 Hover-over or click the **Print** button drop-down menu.

3 Select **Print Preview**. The screen changes to 'Print Preview mode' and the ribbon shows the **Print Preview** tab.

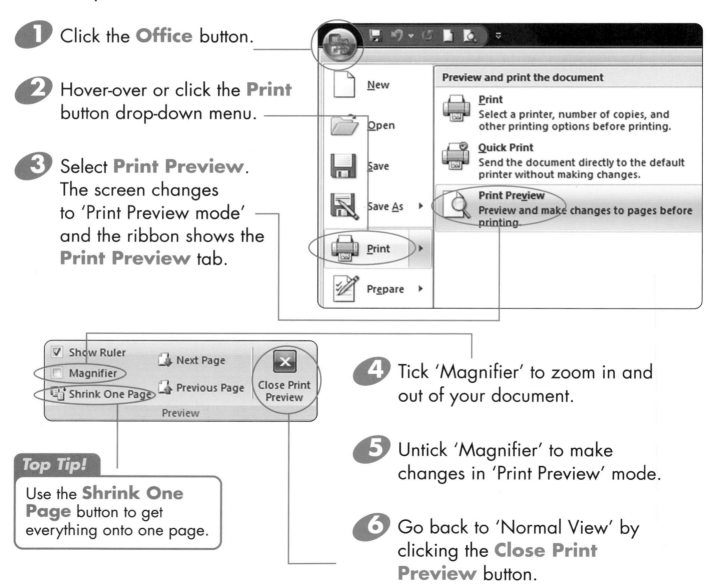

4 Tick 'Magnifier' to zoom in and out of your document.

5 Untick 'Magnifier' to make changes in 'Print Preview' mode.

6 Go back to 'Normal View' by clicking the **Close Print Preview** button.

Top Tip!

Use the **Shrink One Page** button to get everything onto one page.

PROJECT 2 KEEP OUT POSTER

Preview your poster before printing

Checking before printing saves time and money

Before your project is printed, make sure you are happy with it.

1 Print preview your *Keep Out* poster.

2 Check everything looks right.

3 Add blank lines at the top to move the poster text into the middle of the page.

4 Close 'Print preview'.

Is the page the right way around?

Change from **Portrait** to **Landscape**

HOW TO DO IT

A 'Landscape' document is wider than tall. 'Portrait' is taller than wide. Swapping can make your document look better.

1 Click the **Page Layout** tab on the ribbon.

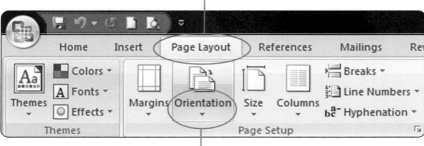

2 Select the **Orientation** button drop-down menu in the 'Page Setup' toolset.

3 Select **Portrait** or **Landscape**.

4 **Orientation** is also available on the 'Print Preview' mode ribbon.

Remember!

Check your changes using 'Print Preview'.

Top Tip!

Landscape folded in half makes a small leaflet.

Set your poster to landscape

Your poster was portrait but looks better landscape

Check which orientation is best for your poster.

1 Set your poster to Landscape.

2 'Print Preview' your poster to check it.

3 Use the **Grow Font** button to make the *KEEP OUT* heading bigger.

4 Change back to Portrait. Shrink the *KEEP OUT* heading to fit the page.

5 Decide which way round is best.

Printing documents

Quick Print and other printing options

HOW TO DO IT

The final step before printing.

1 To print <u>one</u> copy only, click the **Office** button, hover-over **Print**, then select **Quick Print**.

2 For alternatives, select **Print** instead. The 'Print' dialog box appears.

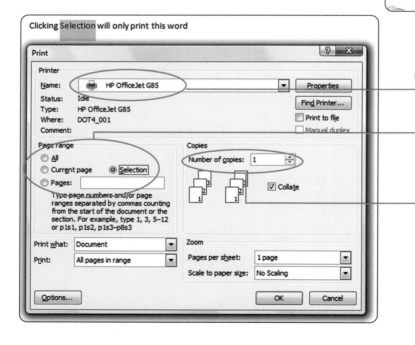

Clicking Selection will only print this word

3 Choose a printer from the **Name** drop-down menu. Choose which pages to print in the **Page range** panel. Type how many copies you want in the **Number of copies** field.

Top Tip!

Ctrl + **P** is the keyboard shortcut for **Print**.

4 Click **OK** to print.

PROJECT 2 KEEP OUT POSTER

Print your poster

Your first **Word** document is ready

USING IT

Print out one copy of your poster, then use the 'Print' dialog box.

1 Select **Quick Print** to print a copy of your poster. Check it looks OK.

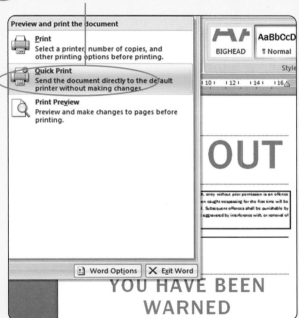

2 Print out two more copies from the 'Print' dialog box.

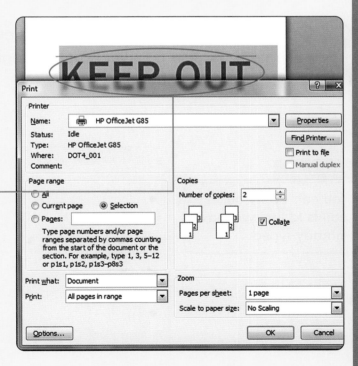

3 Select the *KEEP OUT* heading.

4 Choose 'Selection' and print <u>only</u> this heading from the 'Print' dialog box .

Bullets

Using **Bullet Points**

HOW TO DO IT

Remember!

Use line spacing to space out your list.

'Bullet Points' make easy-to-read lists.

1 Click into a document where you want your list to start.

2 In the 'Paragraph' toolset of the **Home** tab, click the **Bullet** button.

3 A bullet point appears.

4 Type your list. Press the **Enter** key after each item. Notice a bullet point appears at the beginning of each line.

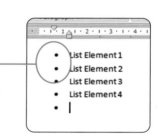

- List Element 1
- List Element 2
- List Element 3
- List Element 4
- |

Top Tip!

You can apply bullet points to lists you have already typed.

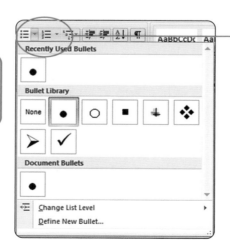

5 Click the **Bullet** button to stop the bullet points.

6 Click the **Bullet** button drop-down menu to select other styles of bullet point.

PROJECT 3 GET YOUR PARTY PLANNED

What do you need for a party?

Use bullet points to make a list

USING IT

Word documents are a great way to make lists.

1 Open a new document.

2 Give your document the heading *My Party* and subtitle *For My party I will need* using different styles.

3 Click the **Bullet** button and list what you need for your party.

4 Click the **Bullet** button and add the second subtitle *These are my guests*.

5 Change the bullet style and list your guests.

My Party

For my party I will need
- Guests
- Music
- Food
- Party games

These are my guests
- Allen Mast
- Kristin Herald
- Vera Deville
- Martin Plascencia
- Johnny Clouse
- Danielle Gupton
- Antonio Gilmer
- Steve Drayton

Challenge!
You can create your own bullet styles. Try using 'Define New Bullet'.

Numbered lists

Using a **Numbered List**

HOW TO DO IT

Remember!
Using lists will automatically add 'Indents'. Use the **Increase Indent** or **Decrease Indent** buttons to change them.

Bullet points add extra space between lines, but numbered lists keep count as well.

1 Start a document.

Top Tip!
If you type *1* then press the **Tab** key, **Word** automatically starts a numbered list.

2 In the 'Paragraph' toolset on the **Home** tab, click the **Numbering** button.

3 1. | will appear.

4 Type your list. Press the **Enter** key after each item.

> 1. First entry
> 2. Second entry
> 3. Third entry
> 4. Fourth entry

5 Click the **Numbering** button to stop numbering.

6 Click the **Numbering** button drop-down menu to use other numbering styles.

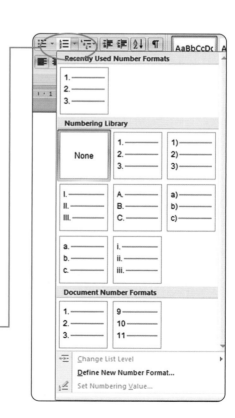

PROJECT 3 GET YOUR PARTY PLANNED

Number your party list

Bullet points are great but numbers help keep count

Use numbering when your list needs an order.

1 Add the subtitle *What food do I want?* to your party plan.

2 Click the **Numbering** button.

3 List the types of food you want.

> *What food do I want?*
>
> 1. Snacks
> 2. Savoury
> 3. Dessert
>
> *What drinks do I want?*
>
> a) Fruit punch
> b) Soda
> c) Fruit juice
> d) Tea & Coffee

4 Stop numbering and add the new subtitle *What drinks do I want?*

5 Change the numbering style to letters and list the drinks you will need.

Lists within lists

Multilevel Lists to add details

HOW TO DO IT

It can help to break down your lists with more detail.

1 Open a new document.

2 In the 'Paragraph' toolset of the **Home** tab, click the **Multilevel List** button drop-down menu.

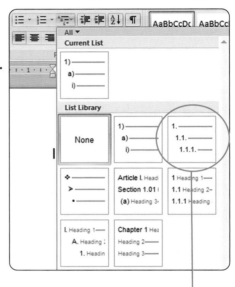

3 Select a style from the 'List Library'.

4 Type a list. Press the **Tab** key to move a level <u>in</u> on the list.

5 Press **Shift** + **Tab** to move <u>out</u> a level.

6 List styles referring to 'Heading' need to be used with 'Heading' styles in the 'Styles' toolset.

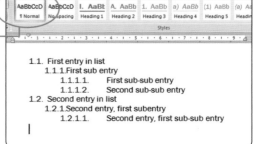

Top Tip!

Select **Clear Formatting** from the 'Styles' toolset drop-down menu to remove list formatting.

PROJECT 3 GET YOUR PARTY PLANNED

Plan your party in more detail

Use multilevel lists to plan your party in greater detail

You have the basic list for your party. Now you need to fill in details.

1 In your party planner click on the first item of your food list.

2 Click the **Multilevel List** button drop-down menu and select a 'Numbered List' style. Do not choose a 'Heading Style' list.

3 At the end of the first line press **Enter** then **Tab.**

4 Add a type of snack, e.g. Chips and Dip, click the **Enter** then **Tab** keys to move in to the next level. List the flavours of that snack.

What food do I want?

1. Snacks
　1.1.Chips and Dip
　　1.1.1. Salsa
　　1.1.2. Guacamole
　　1.1.3. Sour Cream and Chives
　1.2.Popcorn
　　1.2.1. Toffee
　　1.2.2. Butter
2. Savoury

What drinks do I want?

1　　Fruit punch

1.1　Ingredients
4 cups of ginger ale.
2 cups of fruit syrup.
2 cups of pineapple juice.
2 cups of sugar.
1 cup of water.
1 cup of strong, hot tea.
1 cup of lemon juice.

5 Select the drinks list. Select a **Multilevel** style with 'Headings'. Go to the end of the first line and press **Enter**.

6 Select 'Heading 1' from the 'Styles' set. Type a subheading then press **Enter**.

Remember!
Use 'Landscape' orientation to print wide tables.

Tables

Using **Tables** to lay out information

HOW TO DO IT

Word has great tools for quick, good looking tables.

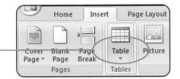

1 From the **Insert** tab, click the **Table** button drop-down menu.

2 Select the number of rows and columns you want. This table has 4 rows and 5 columns.

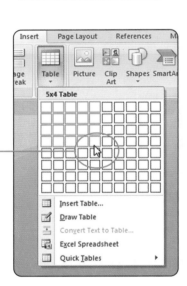

3 The **Design** tab appears on the ribbon. Select a style for your table from the 'Table Styles' toolset.

4 Click into the table and start filling it in.

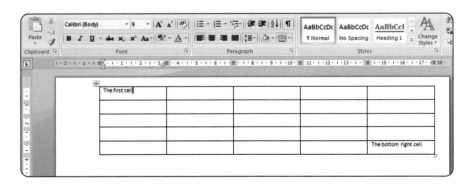

Top Tip!
Pressing the **Tab** key with the cursor in the bottom right cell adds a new row.

PROJECT 3 GET YOUR PARTY PLANNED

Create a checklist of party guests

Use tables to make a party checklist

Tables can be really useful. Where else would you put the party food? (Joke)

USING IT

1 Create a table with 1 row for each guest, a title row and 5 columns.

My party checklist

Guest	Invited	Accepted	Contact Details	Dietary Requirements
Danielle Gupton				
Kristin Herald				
Vera Deville				
Allen Mast				
Martin Plascencia				
Johnny Clouse				
Antonio Gilmer				
Steve Drayton				

2 Apply a table style.

3 Click in the top left cell and type *Guest*, then add headings to each column.

4 Add the guests' names into the first column.

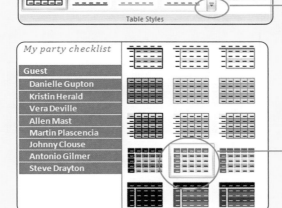

5 Click the 'Table Styles library' dropdown menu to see all styles.

6 Hover-over table styles to preview the look. Choose a table style.

Make your table look good

Table Styles and options

HOW TO DO IT

The **Table Tools-Design** tab gives you options for changing your table.

1 The 'Table Style Options' toolset of the **Design** tab allows you to change the formatting of table styles.

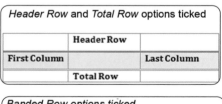

2 Setting the 'First' and 'Last Column' and 'Header Row' options adds emphasis.

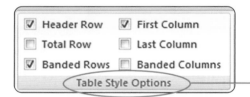

3 The 'Banded Column' and 'Row' options add colour to alternate rows and columns.

4 You can change the colour and borders of cells using the **Shading** button drop-down menu and choosing one.

5 You can add border styles to cells by choosing from the **Borders** button drop-down menu.

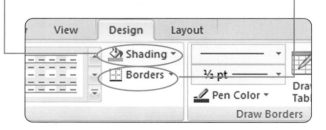

Make your party checklist look good

Style your party checklist for easy reading

USING IT

Your table can look better so information is easier to find.

1 Click into your checklist to bring up the **Table Design** tab on the ribbon.

2 Make sure the 'Header Row', 'First Column' and 'Banded Rows' are the only options selected.

3 Select the *Dietary Requirements* column. Change the background shade colour to dark blue.

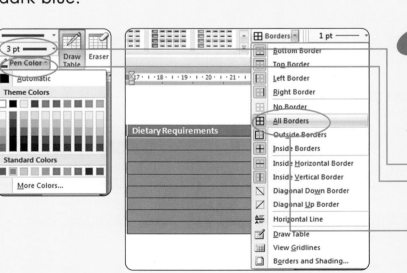

4 Give the column large borders. Click the **Border Line Weight** button drop-down menu to set 3pt. Change the **Pen Color** to white and select **All Borders** from the **Border** button drop-down menu.

Changing your table

Inserting/Deleting/AutoFitting rows and columns

HOW TO DO IT

Tools for designing tables are on the
Layout tab.

Top Tip!

You can click-and-drag the columns in the
ruler at the top of the screen to quickly
change column width.

1 To add a row or column, click in the table where you want to add it.

2 In the 'Rows & Columns'
toolset of the **Layout**
tab, click the
appropriate **Insert**
button.

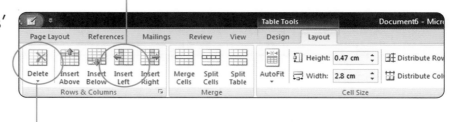

3 To delete a row or column, click on
it then in the 'Rows & Columns'
toolset click on **Delete Table** button.

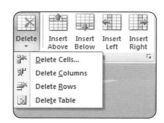

4 Select the delete option you need,
e.g. **Delete Rows**.

5 To change a row or column size, select a cell
within it. Then in the 'Cell Size' toolset of the
Layout tab, increase the height of the row or
width of the column.

6 The **AutoFit Contents** option changes the column
sizes to fit the text in each column. **AutoFit
Window** adjusts the table to fit the page width.

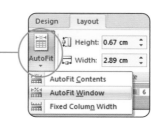

PROJECT 3 GET YOUR PARTY PLANNED

Change your party checklist

Adjusting the columns

Change your checklist to meet your changing needs.

1 Add a column to the end of your table to record the presents your guests bring.

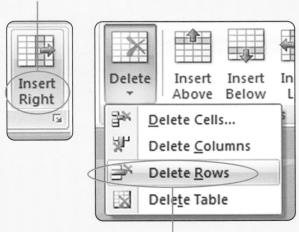

2 Delete one of your guests who cannot come.

3 Make the last column wider.

4 Use **AutoFit Window** to space out the other columns.

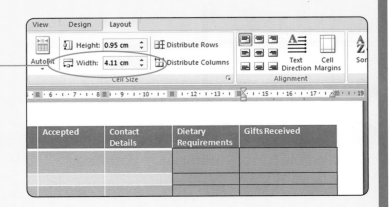

Other table tools

Merging/Splitting Cells and Text Direction.

HOW TO DO IT

You can do many other things with tables. These options help you put the information in the right places.

1 To merge cells into one, select the cells then click the **Merge Cells** button in the 'Merge' toolset of the **Layout** tab.

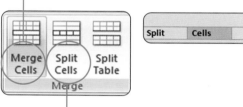

2 To split cells after they have been merged or to add cells within a cell, use the **Split Cells** button.

3 This gives you the option of how many rows and columns you want to split the cell into.

4 You may want to change your text direction, for example if you need text at the top of narrow columns. In the **Layout** tab 'Alignment' toolset, click the **Text Direction** button.

5 Click once to write from top to bottom. Click again to write from bottom to top. Use the **Alignment** buttons to align text within a cell.

PROJECT 3 GET YOUR PARTY PLANNED

Final touches for your checklist

Add merged title rows to your columns

1 Add a column to the left of the checklist.

2 Merge the cells in the column together.

3 Make the text direction bottom to top and type *Guests*. Centre this in the cell.

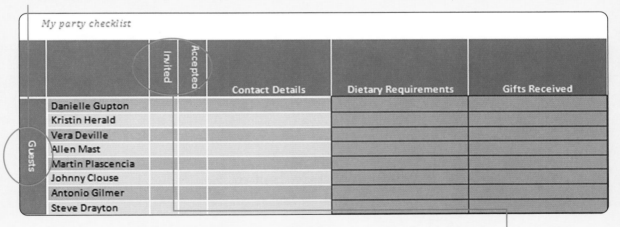

4 Make the *Invited* and *Accepted* columns very narrow.

5 Make the text direction of *Invited* and *Accepted* top to bottom.

Copying

Copy and Paste to save retyping it

HOW TO DO IT

Duplicating text is quicker than typing it again.

1 Select text you want to copy.

This my original text

2 In the 'Clipboard' toolset on the **Home** tab select **Copy**.

3 Move the cursor to where you want the copied text to go.

4 Click the **Paste** button.

5 The copied text appears there.

This my original text

Now I can type some more

And paste - This my original text

Top Tip!

You can 'Copy' and 'Paste' from a website into **Word**.

PROJECT 4 PARTY THANKS

Copy and paste text from your guest list

Use copy and paste to save time

Doing boring jobs can be made quicker using Copy and Paste.

1 Open your party planning document.

Gregorio M. Moore

835 Meadow Drive

Moore, OK 73160

2 Open a new document.
Save it as *Party Thanks*.

3 Start typing a *Thank You* letter. ——— Dear

4 When you need a name from the
party plan, switch to the plan
document and select the name
(turn off the bullets points first).

These are my guests

Allen Mast

Kristin Herald

Vera Deville

5 Copy the name, then switch
back to your letter.

6 Click where you want
the name to go and paste
it into place.

Dear Allen

5 Time saving tools

Moving stuff

> **Top Tip!**
>
> You can click-and-drag selected text around a page.

Moving things around with **Cut** and **Paste Special**

HOW TO DO IT

'Cut' and 'Paste' help you reorganise work.

1 Select the text that you want to move.

> I want to move this word
>
> To this point **here>< **in my document

2 Click **Cut** from the 'Clipboard' toolset. The text disappears.

3 Click where you want the text to go.

> I want to move this
>
> To this point **here>** word **<** in my document

4 Select **Paste**. The text reappears in the new position.

5 If the text is a different <u>style</u> at the new position, use the **Paste** button drop-down menu and select **Paste Special**.

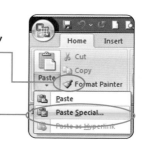

6 Select 'Unformatted Text' and click **OK**. The pasted text is now the same format as surrounding text.

> I want to move this
>
> To this point **here>word** **<** in my document

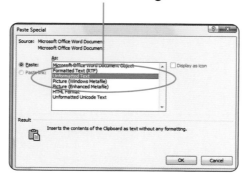

> **Remember!**
>
> You can also use the arrow key on the keyboard to move the cursor.

60

PROJECT 4 PARTY THANKS

Move text in your *Thank You* letter

Use cut and paste to rearrange your *Thank You* letter

Moving text around allows you to see how well different orders of text read.

> Thank you very much for coming to my party. I hope you had as good a time as I did.
> Thanks for the present. I am really looking forward to eating all that candy.

1 Start typing the rest of your *Thank You* letter.

> Thanks for the present. I am really looking forward to eating all that candy.
>
> Thank you very much for coming to my party. I hope you had as good a time as I did.

2 Move the second paragraph to the top.

> Thank you very much for coming to my party. I hope you had as good a time as I did.
> Thanks for the present. I am really looking forward to eating all that candy.

3 Make the text of the top paragraph red.

4 Move the top paragraph back to the bottom. Use 'Paste Special' and the 'Unformatted Text' option to keep the colour the same.

Undoing mistakes

Using the **Undo** and **Repeat** buttons

HOW TO DO IT

It's easy to make a mistake, and just as easy to correct it.
Even if correcting the mistake was a mistake.

Remember!
Use the **Save As** button
to keep up-to-date versions
of your work.

1 Type your name into a document.

2 From the 'Quick Access' toolbar, click the **Undo** button.

3 Your name disappears. To undo more
than one mistake, keep clicking the **Undo** button.

Top Tip!
The keyboard shortcut
for 'Undo' is pressing
the **Ctrl + Z** keys.

4 Or click the **Undo** button drop-down menu.

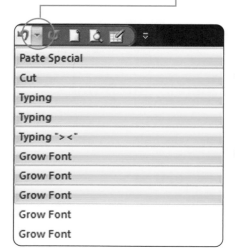

Paste Special
Cut
Typing
Typing
Typing "><"
Grow Font
Grow Font
Grow Font
Grow Font
Grow Font

5 A list of your recent actions appears. Click the
last action you want to undo.

6 If you decide you don't want to undo something
after all, click the **Repeat** button. You can
keep clicking this until you are back to the start.

7 If you haven't undone anything and click
Repeat, it repeats your last action.

PROJECT 4 PARTY THANKS

Get back to somewhere sensible

Moving stuff around can cause problems

USING IT

Let's undo the paragraph swaps on the *Thank You* letter.

1 Click the **Undo** button to swap the paragraphs back.

2 Click the **Undo** button drop-down menu to see all the actions done so far.

3 Undo back to the original plain text letter. Undo to the first 'Clear'.

4 Click the **Repeat** button to get the first colour change back.

> Gregorio M. Moore
> 835 Meadow Drive
> Moore, OK 73160
>
> Dear Allen,
>
> Thank you very much for coming to my party. I hope you had as good a time as I did.
> Thanks for the present. I am really looking forward to eating all that Candy.
>
> Best Regards
>
> Gregorio

Another way of correcting mistakes

Using the **Clipboard**

HOW TO DO IT

The 'Clipboard' allows you to reuse anything that you have copied in *Microsoft Office* and other compatible programs, not just **Word**.

Remember!
If you have moved something, it has been copied first.

1 Open the Party list document.

2 From the 'Clipboard' toolset on the **Home** tab, select the toolset drop-down menu.

3 Find the 'clip' that you want to paste.

4 Click on it to paste it into your document.

Top Tip!
To copy a web address into your document, highlight the address in your browser then right-click and select 'Copy'.

5 Click on this and select to match the surrounding formatting.

PROJECT 4 PARTY THANKS

Copy your guests onto the clipboard

Use the clipboard to create lots of *Thank You* letters

Once the names are on the clipboard, it's easy to churn
out the *Thank You* letters.

1 Open your party
planning document.

2 Select the name of
each guest and
copy it.

3 Open the
Clipboard.

4 Delete the original
name in your letter
and paste a new
name from the
Clipboard.

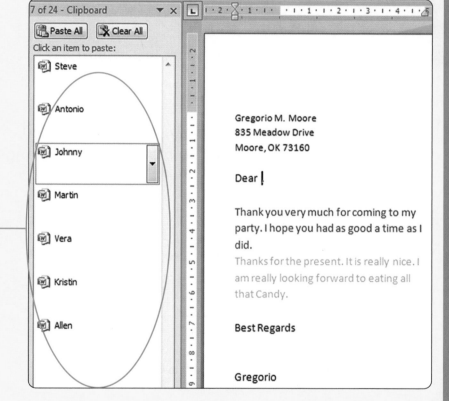

7 of 24 - Clipboard

Paste All   Clear All

Click an item to paste:

Steve

Antonio

Johnny

Martin

Vera

Kristin

Allen

Gregorio M. Moore
835 Meadow Drive
Moore, OK 73160

Dear

Thank you very much for coming to my
party. I hope you had as good a time as I
did.
Thanks for the present. It is really nice. I
am really looking forward to eating all
that Candy.

Best Regards

Gregorio

5 Save the *Thank You* letter with a new
file name. Reopen the original *Thank
You* letter and repeat so you have a
letter for each guest.

Copying styles

Using the **Format Painter**

HOW TO DO IT

We have copied and pasted text.
The 'Format Painter' copies styles.

1 In a document, select text with the format you want to copy.

This is a nice format

This is the text I want to change

2 Click the **Format Painter** button. The selected formatting is copied and the mouse pointer changes to a paintbrush.

3 Move the 'Format Painter' over the text you want to copy the format to.

This is a nice format

This is the text I want to change

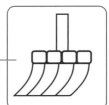

4 Click-and-drag over the text you want to change.

5 Click the **Format Painter** button again to turn it off.

PROJECT 4 PARTY THANKS

Format your *Thank You* letters

Your letters look a bit dull

Use the format painter to change the format of your *Thank You* letters.

1 Select the letter text.

2 Change the font, font size and font colour to *Bradley Hand ITC*, 10 point dark blue text.

Gregorio M. Moore
835 Meadow Drive
Moore, OK 73160

Dear Kristin Allen,

Thank you very much for coming to my party. I hope you had as good a time as I did.
Thanks for the present. It is really nice. I am really looking forward to eating all that candy.

Best Regards

Gregorio

3 Open another letter.

4 Switch back to the first letter.

5 Click in the letter then click the **Format Painter** button.

6 Switch back to the second letter and paste the format over it all.

Gregorio M. Moore
835 Meadow Drive
Moore, OK 73160

Dear Johnny,

Thank you very much for com party. I hope you had as good did.

What's the time?

Inserting the **Date & Time** and **Symbols**

HOW TO DO IT

Word makes life easier with some quick tools.

1 Click where you want the date or time to go.

2 From the 'Text' toolset on the **Insert** tab, click the **Date & Time** button. The 'Date & Time' dialog box appears.

3 Select the format you need.

4 If you want the date or time to be the current one, tick 'Update automatically'.

5 The date and time will update when you reopen the document, or you can click on it and then select the **Update** tab that appears.

6 Click the **Symbol** button drop-down menu on the **Insert** tab.

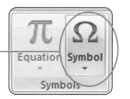

7 Select one of the symbols, e.g. the © symbol from the 'Symbol' dialog box that appears. This will insert it into your text.

PROJECT 4 PARTY THANKS

Insert the date into the *Thank You* letter

Add a date and some symbols to your letters

USING IT

Use the insert options to improve your letters.

1 Open a *Thank You* letter and insert the date after the address.

> Gregorio M. Moore
> 835 Meadow Drive
> Moore, OK 73160
>
> Monday, February 02, 2009
>
> Dear Kristin Allen,

2 Set the date to update automatically in case you print them tomorrow.

3 Add a 'Smiley' symbol.

> Thank you very much for coming to my party. I hope you had as good a time as I did☺.

4 At the bottom add 'Heart' symbols from the *Symbol* font in the **More Symbols** option.

Ω   More Symbols...

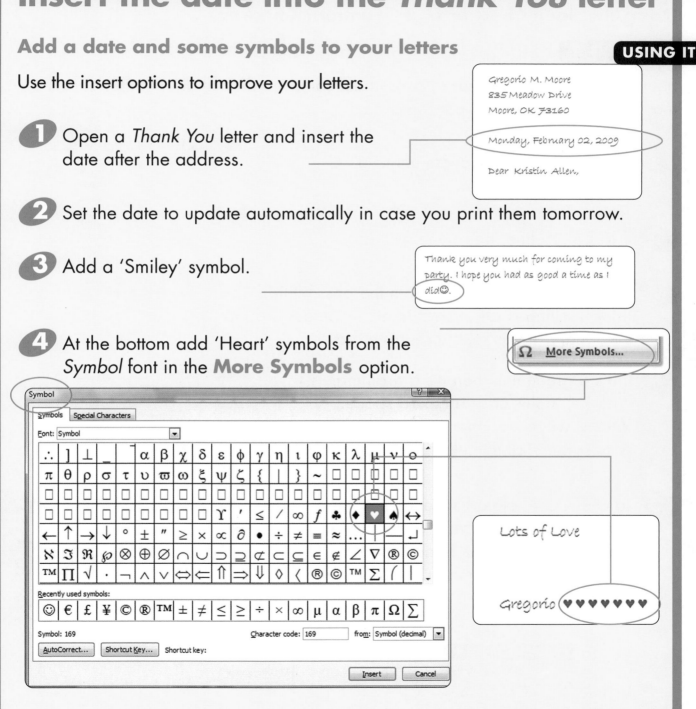

> Lots of Love
>
> Gregorio ♥♥♥♥♥♥

How's your spelling?

Using the **Spell Checker** and **Grammar Checker**

Top Tip!

'Grammar tips' can be hard to get rid of. Use **Word options** from the **Office** button to hide them.

HOW TO DO IT

Squiggly red and green lines appear under some words to show **Word** thinks they may be a spelling or grammar mistake.

1 If a squiggly line appears under a word, right-click on it.

2 If it is a <u>red</u> line, this menu will appear.

3 Choose the right spelling from the possibilities. If the spelling is OK, select **Ignore**. Select 'Add to Dictionary' if you often use this word.

4 If it's a <u>green</u> line then it's a grammar mistake; in this case an extra space. **Word** will either offer you an alternative or tell you what it thinks is wrong.

5 To check a <u>whole</u> document, click the **Spelling & Grammar** button in the **Review** tab. **Word** brings up the 'Spelling and Grammar' dialog box and shows each query.

PROJECT 4 PARTY THANKS

Check your spelling

It's quick and easy to get it right

There is no excuse for bid spulling
with a 'Spell Checker'.

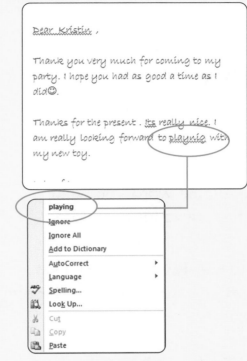

1 Right-click on, and correct anything,
with a red spelling alert.

2 Right-click on, and correct anything, with
a green grammar alert.

3 Double check everything. Bring up the 'Spelling
and Grammar' dialog box and check the whole
document.

5 Time saving tools

Stuck for a word?

Using the **Thesaurus**

HOW TO DO IT

Remember!

Save the original word to the 'clipboard' if you are not convinced you want to change the word.

Word has a great tool for alternatives to words, e.g. *wonderful* and *fantastic* are alternatives to *terrific*.

1 Click on the word you want an alternative for, e.g. *Great*.

2 In the **Review** tab, click the **Thesaurus** button in the 'Proofing' toolset.

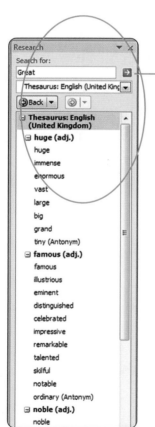

3 The 'Research' dialog box opens.

4 The **Thesaurus** shows alternatives to the word. The different headings depend on the word's meaning.

5 Hover-over the word you want to use; a drop-down menu appears. Click it.

6 Select **Insert** to add that word to your document or **Copy** to use it later. **Look Up** will find more alternatives.

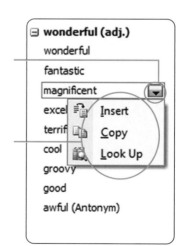

Top Tip!

The thesaurus also suggests the opposites (antonyms) of the word you are looking up. The same as putting 'not' in front of the word.

PROJECT 4 PARTY THANKS

Find new words for *thank you, nice* and *good*

USING IT

It's a bad habit to always use the same word

Make your *Thank You* letter more interesting and expand your vocabulary with the thesaurus.

1 Open a *Thank You* letter.

ch for coming to my
ad as good a time as I

Research ▼ ✕

Search for:

good ➡

Thesaurus: English (UK) ▼

◄ Back | ▼   ◄ | ▼

⊟ **Thesaurus: English (UK)**

⊞ **high-quality (adj.)**
⊞ **decent (adj.)**
⊞ **enjoyable (adj.)**
⊞ **skillful (adj.)**
⊞ **helpful (adj.)**
⊞ **nice (adj.)**
⊞ **well-behaved (adj.)**
⊞ **benefit (n.)**

2 Click on a common word like *good*.

3 Check the list of alternatives.

⊟ **nice (adj.)**
nice
fine
lovely ▼
clear
mild

4 Hover-over the one you want to use and insert it in your letter.

for coming to my
as lovely a time as

Finding out more

Remember!

You can also use *Yahoo!* or *Google*, and copy information into your document.

Word links to the internet to help Research your work

HOW TO DO IT

The **Research** button finds information on the internet.

Endangered Animals

1 Select the word(s) you want more information about.

2 Click the **research** button on the **Review** tab.

Top Tip!

Clicking while pressing the **Alt** key automatically opens the **Research** window.

3 You will get a list of websites. Select the one you want to check.

4 Click on a link to see that web page.

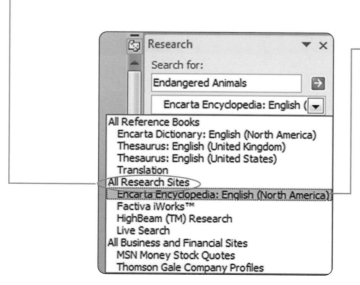

PROJECT 4 PARTY THANKS

Use Research to find out about your presents

USING IT

The internet has lots of information for you

The **Research** button makes it easy to show you liked your presents.

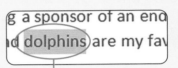

1 Click on the word you want to study.

2 Look up the word on a research site.

3 Find some interesting information from the links.

4 Use your new knowledge to improve your letter.

Research

Search for:

dolphins

Encarta Encyclopedia: English (

Back

☐ Encarta Encyclopedia: English (North America)

☐ Dolphin (aquatic mammal)

Dolphin (aquatic mammal), fast-swimming mammal belonging to the order Cetacea, which also includes whales and porpoises. Sleek and powerful...

Article—Encarta Encyclopedia

I. Introduction

II. Physical Description

III. Behavior

IV. Types of Dolphins

V. Threats to Dolphins

☐ **Related items**

Toothed Whales, including dolphins and porpoises

Bottlenose Dolphin, most studied species

Killer Whale, largest dolphin

Pilot Whale, member of the ocean dolphin family

Porpoise, closed related toothed whale

anatomy and physiology

art and mythology of ancient Greece

☐ **Media**

Dolphin Quick Facts

Thanks for the present. It is really nice. I like being a sponsor of an endangered animal and dolphins are my favourite. Did you know that they can swim as fast as 25mph and dive 200 feet or more?

A picture is worth a 1000 words

Adding **Pictures**

HOW TO DO IT

With digital cameras and the internet it's easy to put pictures into a document.

Remember!

You can copy and paste pictures to move them around.

1 Click where you want a picture to go.

2 From the **Insert** tab, click the **Picture** button. The 'Insert Picture' dialog box appears.

Top Tip!

Use the **Views** button on the 'Insert Picture' dialog box to see available pictures.

3 Find a picture on your computer then click **Insert**. The picture appears in your document.

4 Click-and-drag the <u>corners</u> to change the size of your picture. Click-and-drag the <u>green dot</u> to rotate it.

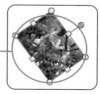

PROJECT 5 SCHOOL FAIR POSTER

School fair poster

Use pictures to smarten up a poster

Pictures are excellent for making your poster eye-catching.

1 Open a new document.

2 Insert a picture into your poster.

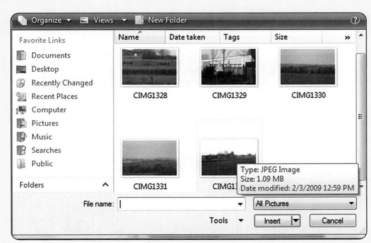

3 Make the picture smaller.

4 Rotate the picture to make it look whacky.

Maximise picture impact

Changing **Picture Styles**

HOW TO DO IT

The **Picture Tools-Format** tab has lots of options for styling your picture.
Add borders, picture effects or change picture shape.

1 To add a border, click on the picture
and select a border from the 'Picture
Styles' toolset.

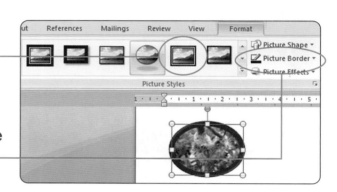

2 Change picture frame colour using the
Picture Border button.

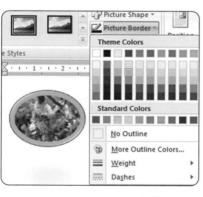

3 Make the picture frame
an interesting shape
using the **Picture
Shape** button.

4 The **Picture Effects**
button adds cool effects.

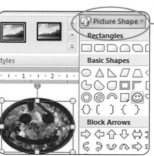

PROJECT 5 SCHOOL FAIR POSTER

Make the picture stand out

A good frame defines a picture

Make the picture stand out against the white background.

1 Click on your picture.

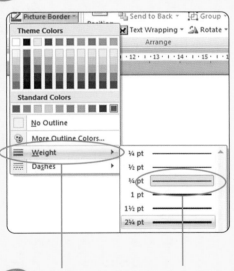

Challenge!
Can you use the **Crop** button to reduce your picture to just the part you need?

2 Give it a cloud shaped frame from the **Picture Shape** options.

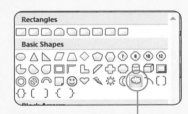
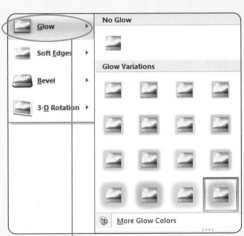

3 Give the frame a colourful border.

4 Select a **Glow** picture effect.

Clip Art

Word comes with cartoons called Clip Art

Top Tip!

Use **Cut** and **Paste** to move things around, or click-and-drag.

HOW TO DO IT

'Clip Art' are pictures built into **Word** for you to use. There is also a library of 'Clip Art' on the internet if you need more.

1 Click into the document where you want the 'Clip Art' to go.

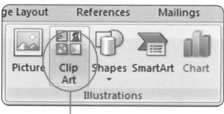

2 From the **Insert** tab 'Illustrations' toolset, click the **Clip Art** button.

3 The 'Clip Art' dialog box opens.

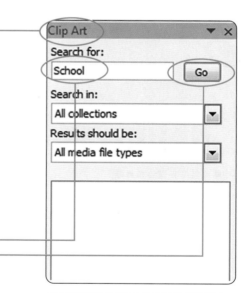

4 Type what sort of picture you want in the **Search for** field, then click **Go**.

5 If you don't like the pictures shown, click the **Search in** field drop-down menu, tick 'Web Collections' then click the **Go** button again.

6 To use a 'Clip Art' picture, click on it.

PROJECT 5 SCHOOL FAIR POSTER

Add a few Clip Art pictures

Cartoons are always fun

USING IT

Clip Art is available on almost any subject.
Use it to brighten up your poster.

1 Search for Clip Art related to your school fair.

2 Click on the poster where you want the
Clip Art to go.

3 Insert the picture.

4 Resize, rotate and add borders to match
the other picture.

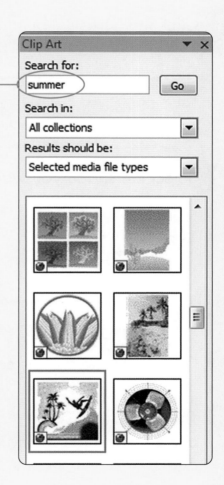

Inserting shapes

Arrows, speech bubbles and other shapes

HOW TO DO IT

As well as Clip Art, **Word** has shapes you can use.

1 Click the **Shapes** button drop-down menu.

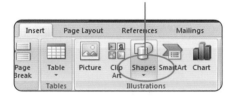
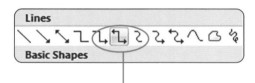

2 Select the shape you want to use.

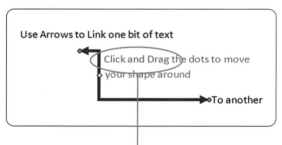

3 Click-and-drag the shape to where you want it.

4 The **Drawing Tools-Format** tab opens on the ribbon, allowing you to change the shapes, colours, widths and style of the shapes.

PROJECT 5 SCHOOL FAIR POSTER

Add a speech bubble to the picture

Use shapes to customise your pictures

Shapes allow you to draw on your poster.

1 Add a square speech bubble 'Callout' shape to your poster.

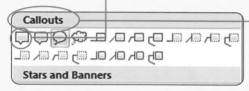

2 Click-and-drag it so the speech bubble is coming out of the picture.

3 Click into the speech bubble and start typing.

4 Insert an arrow between your picture and the Clip Art.

5 Use a 'Shape Style' from the **Format** tab to increase the size of the arrow.

Text boxes

Moving text around with **Text Boxes**

HOW TO DO IT

'Text Boxes' are a smart way of adding blocks of text.

1 From the **Insert** tab, click the **Text Box** button drop-down menu.

2 Select a text box style. This one's called *Austere Sidebar*.

3 Click into the text box and type your text.

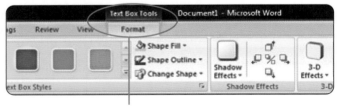

4 The **Text Box Tools-Format** tab opens so you can change the format of the text box.

5 Click-and-drag the text box to move it or the corners to change the size.

> **Remember!**
>
> Click back on the **Home** tab to change the font and paragraph style of your text.

Top Tip!

Text boxes can go anywhere that the 'Insert' point can go. If you have a new document, press the **Enter** key until you get to the bottom of the page.

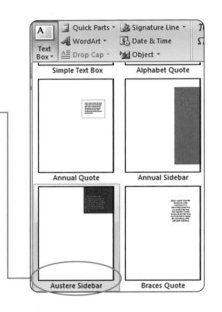

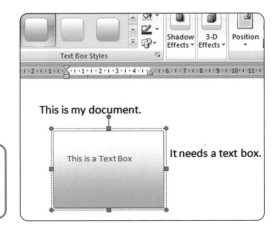

PROJECT 5 SCHOOL FAIR POSTER

Add a text box to your poster

Add a text box with details of the fair

A text box helps distinguish text from the rest of the document.

1 Click at the bottom of your poster.

2 Insert a text box. Use the *Mod Quote* style.

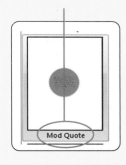

3 Insert the date and time of fair into the text box.

4 Use the **Format** button to change the
style to match the rest of your poster.
Add a 3-D Effect to jazz it up.

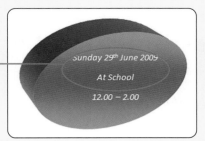

Outstanding text effects

Insert **WordArt** into the document

HOW TO DO IT

'WordArt' allows colourful effects for your text.

Top Tip!

Press **Delete** to get rid of your 'WordArt'.

1 Open a new document.

2 From the **Insert** tab, click the **WordArt** button drop-down menu.

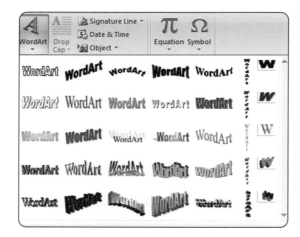

3 Select a 'WordArt' style.

4 The 'Edit WordArt Text' dialog box appears. Type the text to be changed into 'WordArt'. Click **OK**.

5 The **WordArt Tools-Format** tab opens, giving you formatting options.

6 Click [Edit Text] to edit your text.

Remember!

Hover-over a style option to preview it.

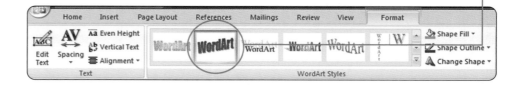

PROJECT 5 SCHOOL FAIR POSTER

Add a wild title to your poster

Use WordArt to give your poster a big title

WordArt can make your text look amazing.

1 Click in your poster where you want your title.

2 Select a 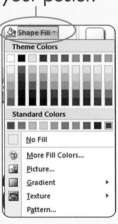 style and type your title in the dialog box.

3 Modify the style and click-and-drag the corners to make it fit your poster.

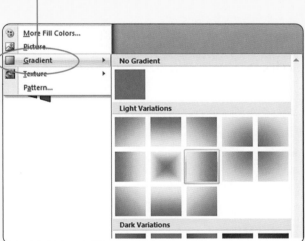

Adding text around inserts

How to **Wrap** text around pictures

HOW TO DO IT

Pictures and WordArt use a single line in your document. 'Wrapping' lets you make them part of the text.

1 Click on the object you want to wrap text around.

2 From the **Format** tab, click the **Text Wrapping** button drop-down menu.

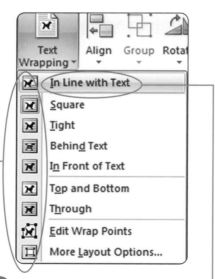

3 Select a 'Wrap' option. The default is **In Line with Text**. The icons show you how the text wrap will look.

4 These are some 'Wrap' options.

Square

This is wrapping the ... square around object

Tight

This is ... tight wrapping around the ... object

In Front of Text

This is ... in front of text

PROJECT 5 SCHOOL FAIR POSTER

Wrap text around the poster's text box

Use text wrap to run text around the 'fair details' text box on the poster

Without wrapping, inserted objects such as WordArt and text boxes get in the way of the main document.

1 Click on the text box.

2 Set wrap to **Tight**.

3 Click on the poster to the left of the text box.

4 Type out the attractions at your fair.

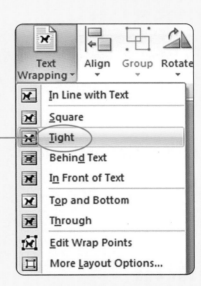

A white background can be dull

Change your document's background colour or make a picture the background

> **Top Tip!**
>
> You can also use coloured paper in your printer.

You can add effects to the background of your document.

1 From the **Page Layout** tab, select the **Page Color** button.

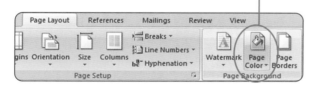

2 Select a background colour.

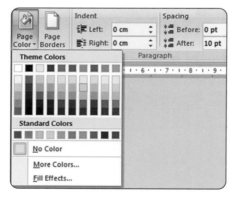

3 To add effects or use a picture, select **Fill effects** instead. The 'Fill effects' dialog box appears.

> **Remember!**
>
> Page backgrounds look great but are just for looking at on screen. They don't print out.

4 The 'Gradient' effect changes the background colour shades.

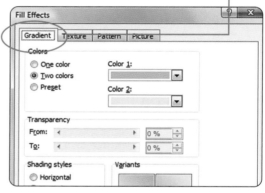

5 To make a picture the background, click the **Picture** tab, click the **Select Picture...** button and choose a picture on your computer.

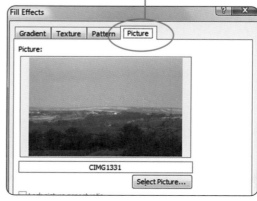

Add a gradient background to the poster

USING IT

A blue shaded background will have an impact

It won't print, but looks great on screen.

1 Click the **Page Layout** tab and the **Page Color** button drop-down menu.

2 Bring up the 'Fill Effects' dialog box and click the **Gradient** tab.

3 Create a 'Two colours' gradient with two different light blues.

4 Select 'From corner' in the 'Shading Styles' panel and select a variant. Click **OK**.

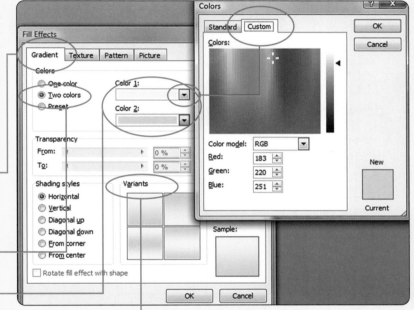

A classy background option

Using **Watermarks**

HOW TO DO IT

'Watermarks' are faint background text or pictures, as on bank notes. These <u>do</u> print out.

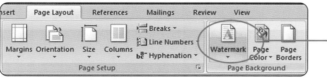

1 Click the **Watermark** button drop-down menu on the **Page Layout** tab.

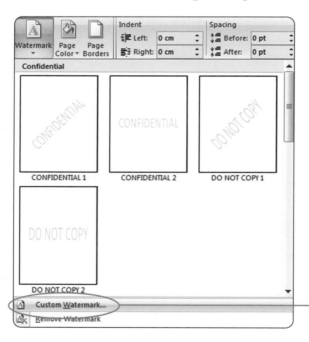

2 The standard 'Watermarks' are a bit boring. Select **Custom Watermark**. The 'Printed watermark' dialog box appears.

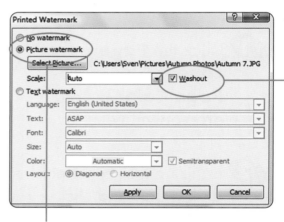

3 To add a picture as a watermark, select the 'Picture watermark' option, then 'Select Picture'. 'Washout' makes sure you can read text on top of the Watermark.

This is a washed out picture

Top Tip!

Use smaller pictures with plenty of contrast for best effects.

PROJECT 5 SCHOOL FAIR POSTER

Add a picture as a watermark

Use a picture of your school or class

Fill the poster background with a picture watermark.

1 Click the **Watermark** button on the **Page Layout** tab.

2 Select **Custom Watermark** from the drop-down menu.

3 Select the picture you want to use on your computer.

4 Click **Apply** to preview it, then click the **Close** button.

5 Change 'Washout' and 'Scale' to see what works best.

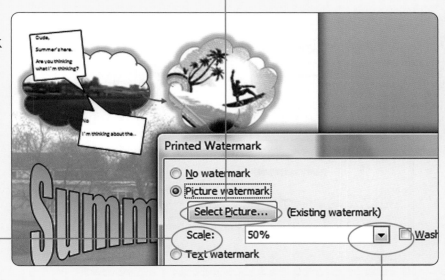

Frame your work

Adding **Borders** to documents

HOW TO DO IT

A good border improves the look of some documents.

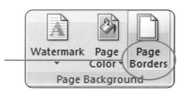

1 Click the **Page Borders** button on the **Page Layout** tab. The 'Borders and Shading' dialog box appears.

2 Set the 'Page Border', style, colour and width options. Check different combinations in the 'Preview' panel.

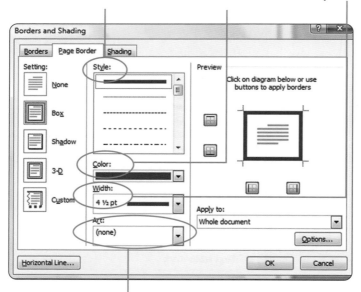

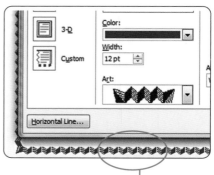

3 The 'Art' drop-down menu lets you make fancy borders.

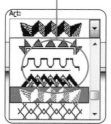

PROJECT 5 SCHOOL FAIR POSTER

Add a border to your poster

Absolutely the final touch

Adding a border frames the poster nicely.

1 Click the **Page Borders** button and bring up the 'Borders and Shading' dialog box.

2 Add a border in a colour that matches everything else.

3 Try using an 'Art' style.

4 Save and print your poster.

Judging a book by its cover

Using the **Standard Cover Pages**

Word comes with this option to help beginners make their work look good.

> **Remember!**
> You can use formatting tools in the cover page fields.

1 Open a new document. Click the **Cover Page** button on the **Insert** tab.

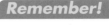

2 Select a cover page style.

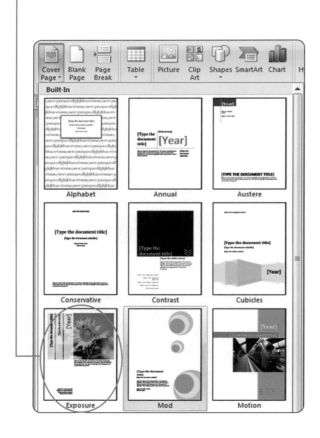

3 Type into the places indicated to complete your cover page.

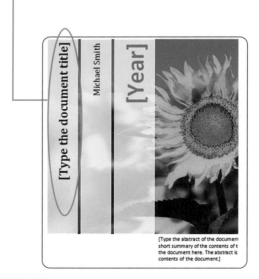

> **Top Tip!**
> Type a **Space** to hide any fields you don't need.

PROJECT 6 SPORTS DAY PROGRAMME

Create a cover page for your programme

USING IT

Use a standard cover page to start

Using a standard cover page will give your programme a professional look.

1 Open a new document.

2 Save it as *Sports Day Programme*.

3 Add a standard cover page using the *Annual* style.

4 Add the name of your school, the date of the sports day and other important information in the fields.

Challenge!

Cover pages are made using standard **Word** formatting. Click on each element to see how it's done.

Setting page margins

How much space do you want at the edge of your page?

HOW TO DO IT

Changing 'Margins' helps your work fit onto a page.

1 'Margins' are set from the **Page Layout** tab.

2 There are several standard schemes.

3 If these do not suit, select **Custom Margins**.

Custom Margins...

4 The 'Page Setup' dialog box allows you to set the margins exactly.

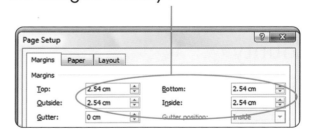

Top Tip!

Most printers can't print to the edge of the paper so don't make the margins too small.

PROJECT 6 SPORTS DAY PROGRAMME

Set the size of your programme

Make your programme fit the page

USING IT

Set the margins on the programme.

1 On the first page of your programme, type out the timetable of events.

2 On the second page, list who is running in each race.

3 On the third page, add a plan of the school and the sports ground.

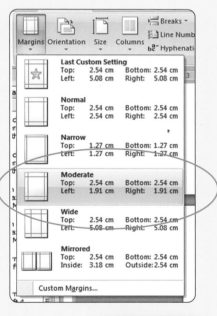

4 Change the margins to moderate.

5 Preview your work.

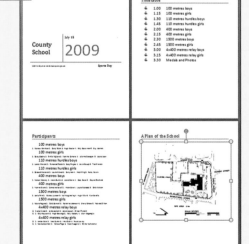

Challenge!

In the 'Custom Margins' option on the **Margins** button drop-down menu you can set 'Multiple Pages' per page to create a booklet. Can you use this for your programme?

Breaking up your work

Adding **Page Breaks**

HOW TO DO IT

Adding 'Page Breaks' stops you worrying about pages shifting as you add text.

Remember!

'Many Pages' in **Print Preview** helps you see all your pages at once.

1 From the **Insert** tab, click the **Page Break** button.

2 If you want to change the layout between pages, you need to choose the **Section Breaks** option.

3 In the **Page Layout** tab, click the **Breaks** button drop-down menu.

4 This gives you several options.

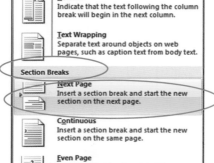

5 Select the **Next page** option to allow you to switch between *portrait* and *landscape*.

Top Tip!

The Keyboard command for page break is **Ctrl + Enter**.

PROJECT 6 SPORTS DAY PROGRAMME

Add page and section breaks between pages

USING IT

Page breaks will stop your programme text moving around

Page breaks and section breaks are very important when you are laying out a multi-page document.

1 Add a page break at the end of the timetable of events.

2 Add more text to the end of the timetable. The next page stays as it was.

3 Add a section break at the end of the third page.

4 Make the fourth page landscape.

Drinks and Snacks w throughout the day

Participants

100 metres boys

1. Mathew Kennison 2. Darryl Blunk 3. H

Participants

100 metres boys
1. Mathew Kennison 2. Darryl Blunk 3. Hugh Keader 4. Kelly Bowerman 5. Guy Adamek

100 metres girls
1. Cerdu Sadna 2. Emilia Migliore 3. Karivina Cerrone 4. Julianne Castagna 5. Louisa Lepe

110 metres hurdles boys
1. Lonnie Kinsaird 2. Fernando Fiddler 3. Cody Pingree 4. Javier Goudy 5. Ted Kherman

110 metres hurdles girls
1. Deborah Kardvick 2. Laurie Mason 3. Berryman 4. Heidi Kling 5. Kathy Marvin

400 metres boys
1. Nelson Manisely 2. Jessie Dumire 3. Jessie Briant 4. Cody Devau 5. Clayton Eberhard

400 metres girls
1. Yvonne Olivera 2. Constance Sprull 3. Helen Orne 4. Louise Svoboda 5. Della Waldon

1500 metres boys
1. Jamie Prim 2. Mathew Landon 3. Nall Kaughtraling 4. Hugh Vilar 5. Kurt Cardilla

1500 metres girls
1. Valerie Pagano 2. Della Conuell 3. Katherine Johansen 4. Cheryl Grace 5. Yolanda Clifton

4x400 metres relay boys
4. 1. Julio Waldie 2. Jamie Jaohan 3. Jessie Leask 4. Clinton Tamplin

4x400 metres relay girls
4. 1. Kelly Wayworth 2. Hugh Bevaridge 3. Kelly Mobberly 4. Allan Mcgonagle

A Plan of the School

Creating text columns

Lay your work out in columns

HOW TO DO IT

Text columns makes reading easier. Newspapers do this.

Remember!
Small fonts help get lots of information on a page.

1 Click where you want the columns to start.

2 If this is not at the beginning of a document, add a section break, otherwise the whole document will change into columns.

3 In the **Page Layout** tab, click the **Columns** button drop-down menu.

4 Click on a standard column format, or select **More Columns** to set up something special.

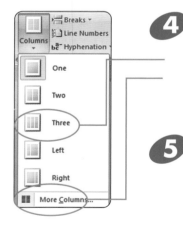

5 Add another section break and select the **Columns** button drop-down menu to return the document to one column.

This is my document

After a section break I now have three columns. They are filled with text. After a section break I now have three After a section break I now ave three columns. They are filled with text. After a section break I now have three columns. They are filled with text. After a

section break I now have three columns. They are filled with text. After a section break I now have three columns. They are filled with text. After a section break I now have three columns. They are filled with text. After a section break I now have

three columns. They are filled with text. After a section break I now have three columns. They are filled with text. After a section break I now have three columns. They are filled with text

This is another section break

Top Tip!
Use the **Hyphenation** button to break up long words in your narrow columns.

PROJECT 6 SPORTS DAY PROGRAMME

Add columns to your programme

Use columns on a page with lots of text

You can write lots about each race.

1 Add a 'Next Page' section break. at the start of the last page.

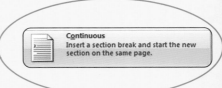

Section Breaks

Next Page
Insert a section break and start the new section on the next page.

2 Add a new title to the page and press the **Enter** key.

3 Add a 'Continuous' section break.

Continuous
Insert a section break and start the new section on the same page.

4 Click the **Columns** button drop-down menu and select **More Columns** to bring up the 'Columns' dialog box. Create four columns on the page.

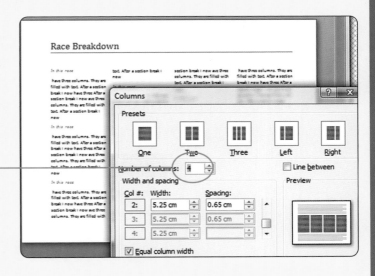

Race Breakdown

Columns

Presets

One   Two   Three   Left   Right

Number of columns: 4   ☐ Line between

Width and spacing   Preview

Col #:   Width: Spacing:
2:    5.25 cm   0.65 cm
3:    5.25 cm   0.65 cm
4:    5.25 cm

☑ Equal column width

Adding comments

Comments that are seen but not printed

Remember!

You can also print your work and write on it.

HOW TO DO IT

'Comments' let other people know why you have done something on group projects.

1 Select text you wish to add a 'Comment' to.

2 In the **Review Tab** click the **New Comment** button.

3 A red marker and comment bubble appear. Type your comment into the bubble.

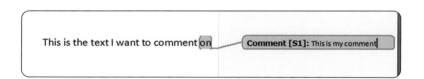

This is the text I want to comment on — Comment [S1]: This is my comment

4 Use the delete comment button to delete a selected comment or all comments on a document.

Top Tip!

For comments that <u>do</u> get printed out, use footnotes.

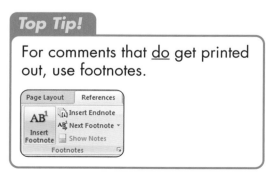

PROJECT 6 SPORTS DAY PROGRAMME

Add comments to the programme

Use comments to explain your thinking

Projects like a sports day programme are often done by several people.

1 Add a comment to the timetable.

2 Click on the picture of the school grounds. Add a comment to it.

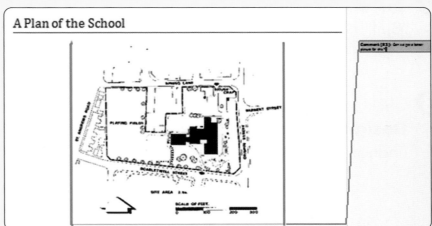

3 Add another comment and then delete it.

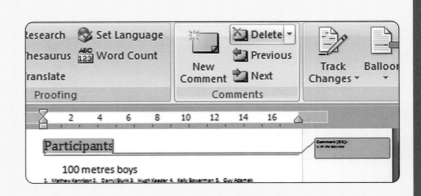

Headers and footers

Add the same text to the top or bottom of every page

HOW TO DO IT

'Headers' and 'Footers' help keep your document together.

1 In the **Insert** tab, click the **Header** or **Footer** buttons.

2 You will then be presented with a series of 'Built-In' options.

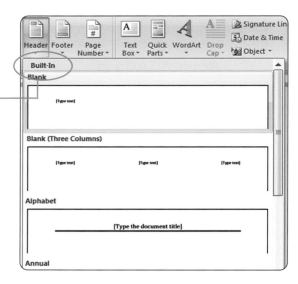

3 Click one. The **Header & Footer Tools-Design** tab opens, allowing you to change the style.

4 Type into the fields indicated. [Type text]

5 Many of the built in headers and footers have automatic page numbering.

PROJECT 6 SPORTS DAY PROGRAMME

Add a programme header

Use the built in styles to add a header

A title and page number on every page
will help people reading the programme.

Annual

[Type the d

1 Open the programme.

2 Click the **Header** button and add a header. We used the *Annual*
style for the cover.

3 Notice that **Word** uses the title and date
from the cover. Because we used section breaks
earlier, you need to add the header to each
section separately.

County School | 2009

4 Insert a picture or ClipArt into the header.

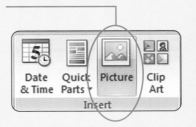

5 Click the **Close header and footer** button to return to the main
document.

6 Use the **Print Preview** button to check your work.

Page numbering

Add the **Page Number** using a nice style

HOW TO DO IT

Page numbers help the reader know their position in a document.

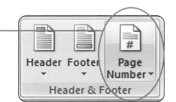

1 From the **Insert** tab, click the **Page Number** button
drop-down menu.

2 Decide where the page number needs to go.

3 The **Current Position** option adds page numbering
from the cursor onwards.

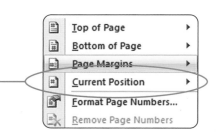

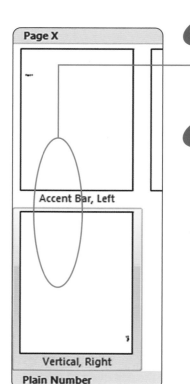

4 Select a page number
style from the list
available.

5 Format the page numbers
using the **Text Box
Formatting** button. You
can add shapes and
backgrounds or click-and-
drag them around if you
have chosen the **Page
Margins** option.

Top Tip!

You can create a Table
of Contents including
page numbers if your
Heading styles are
consistent. See the
References tab.

PROJECT 6 SPORTS DAY PROGRAMME

Add page numbers

Explore page numbering options

Add a page number to the *Sports Day Programme* and use text box styling options.

1 Insert page numbering into the programme.

2 Select the [Page Margins ▶] **Page Margins** option.

3 Select a 'With Shapes' style.

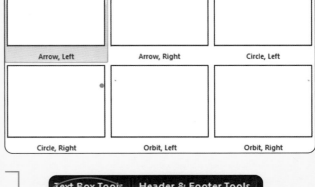

4 Use the **Text Box Tools-Format** tab to change the shape colour to match the rest of the programme. Change the shape to a **Callout**.

5 Move the page number shape by click-and-dragging.

Using the help menus

Remember!
Press the **F1** key to pop up 'Help'.

Other sources of help

Word has help built in. If you are connected to the internet there is more.

1 To get 'Help', click the ❓ icon.

2 Type your question into the search field.

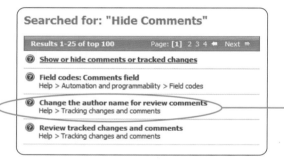

3 If you aren't on the internet, 'Help' will show the built in answers to your question.

4 If you are connected to the internet, 'Help' will also show links to demonstrations and videos.

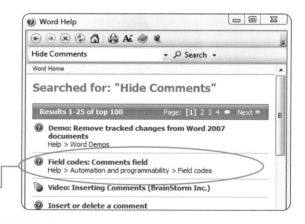

Top Tip!

Don't be afraid to experiment. Use **Undo** and save copies to avoid permanent mistakes.

PROJECT 7 USING THE HELP MENUS

Get yourself some help!

Did we lose you on one of the projects?

There are lots more tools to look at. Use **Help** to find out about them.

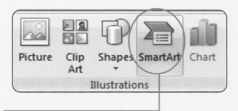

1 Search for help on the **SmartArt** button.

2 How can you add a 'Hyperlink'?

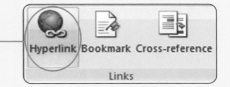

3 How do you hide 'Comments'?

4 How can you stop other people changing your document?

i Index